Southword 43

Southword is published
by Southword Editions
an imprint of the
Munster Literature Centre
Frank O'Connor House
84 Douglas Street
Cork City T12 X802
Ireland

www.munsterlit.ie

@MunLitCentre

/southwordjournal

/munsterliteraturecentre

#Southword

Issue 43
ISBN 978-1-905002-98-6

Editor
Patrick Cotter

Fiction Editor
Billy O'Callaghan

Production
James O'Leary

Thank you to Anne Kennedy for her technical assistance

The opinions expressed by contributing writers are not necessarily representative of the publisher's or editors' opinions

Cover image: *'Little Worlds'* by Anne Kennedy

The Munster Literature Centre is a grateful recipient of funding from

Comhairle Cathrach Chorcaí
Cork City Council

CONTENTS

Poems	**7**	Amy Woolard
Fiction	**12**	Gerard Beirne
Poems	**21**	Kevin Cahill Lorraine McArdle Róisín Ryan
Photo Essay	**25**	John Minihan
Fiction	**37**	Jose Varghese
Poems	**45**	Tomás de Faoite Daragh Byrne Jane Robinson Róisín Leggett Bohan Geraldine Mitchell
Fiction	**52**	Patrick Holloway
Poems	**58**	Michael Farry David S. Higdon Julia Deakin David Murphy Fran Lock
Photo Essay	**63**	Rebecca Moseman
Poems	**76**	Trelawney Louise G. Cole John Paul Davies

Fiction	**80**	Donal McLaughlin
Poems	**85**	Claire Hennessy
		Donna Morton
		Tracy Gaughan
		Jess Smith
		Leah Saint Marie
		Afric McGlinchey
		Martin Mc Carthy
Fiction	**93**	Deirdre Crowley
Poems	**98**	Regi Claire
		Lani O'Hanlon
		Sinéad McClure
Fiction	**101**	Alan McCormick
Poems	**113**	Olaitan Humble
		James McDermott
Fiction	**118**	Kay Sexton
Poems	**123**	Nwanne Agwu
		Meg Eden
		Greg Delanty
		Pragya Gogoi
		Fred Johnston
		Thomas McCarthy
Interview	**132**	Thomas McCarthy

Please Subscribe

By subscribing, you will receive new issues of *Southword* straight from the printers, as quickly as we will ourselves. Your subscription will also help to provide us with the resources to make *Southword* even better.

Rates for two issues per year:

Ireland, UK, North America, Australia, New Zealand	€20 *postage free*
Rest of Europe	€24 *postage free, tax-inclusive*
Rest of the World	€30 *postage included*

For subscriptions and renewals visit www.munsterlit.ie – payment accepted by PayPal.

Southword may also be purchased issue-by-issue through Amazon outlets worldwide and select book shops in Ireland, the UK, Europe and the USA.

THREE POEMS
Amy Woolard

BARTENDER'S CURSE

May the stamp inked onto the back of your
Hand at the door always be the name of

Your nemesis. May it last into the daylight &
For days then-on. May you sleep weirdly

On your hand so the name becomes
Unwashably printed on your cheek.

May your house be mirrorless & too
Bright. Sweetheart, take a fine look at

Yourself. Guilt is just the fear of having fallen
Out of love w/your ghosts. Your ghosts

Are a tonic. May they fool the desert
Of your morning mouth. May the erased

Evening come back to you like a split hand
Of blackjack. May your longing have opened

A tab & forgotten to pay. There are not
Enough dishes you could possibly wash

That would settle what's owed.
May you endlessly clock in to

This world. May your love leave
You pennies on the table.

Last

Our love loves the same way news must feel
When it travels. In the South: it's not the heat, it's

The leaving each other, infinitum, how the bed is
Undone as my witched hair, how the morning presses

Its palm into my palm while I watch you
Dress. How you deadline the door, hold

Your face like a drink you ordered though
You weren't thirsty. It's the humidity

Of not touching. When I tell you
I miss you what I'm really saying is

I hope my sister never dies. *An absence
Of evidence, rather than evidence of absence.*

Dear last love: the afterward is already
Now. Each morning a new same hits

Home. Days go by like the past
Owners of a house circling the old

Neighborhood—there is no azalea, no
Blue pickup, no glass door corsaged

With light. With our hands we cover our
Mouths to keep the lungs from leaving us

When a sorrow hits them. Like sorrows there are
More cardinals than trees to hold them close, but

Still they stay. It's the leaving each other
Alone. I'm saying it's how a body can be

Had. With our hands we tuck back the
Impossible falling long across our faces.

We palm the soft dogs' softer ears so we can
Better dream of them when they're gone.

ELECTRIC WORD LIFE

I had a skirt I loved so much I only
Wore it to sleep. What I mean is

I only wore it to wake. I
Mean the morning & me like

A torn over-easy egg, admix
Of erasure & astonishment &

Salt, peeling off the dream in long
Strips of masking tape from the fact

Of the window trim. The skirt
Peeling off from the fact of our

Hands. Is astonishment even the way
To say the membrane between

Us, is it loose in me like a bird who
Makes a classic mistake & traps itself

Inside, mapping the house like a county
Fair. Love, I opened every window &

Door to give it the best chance to
Leave. What I mean is the first time we

Clocked each other, it was I knew for
Life, the way a dog yawns with

His whole body & once when I
Asked you said it felt like a shoal like

A thousand turnings but exactly
All at once & I couldn't help

But remember the tv reporter who
Began weeping on air in the middle

Of his sentence, unsheltered
By his own breaking news.

Bad-assing With Nick Cave In A Blue Cadillac On A Black Friday Night
Gerard Beirne

Kid pulls up next to me. Rolls the window down. "Get in."

And I do.

Tells me straight away that he's Nick Cave.

"You don't look the first thing like Nick Cave," I tell him.

He revs up the engine. "Nick Cave don't look like Nick Cave." Pulls back into the traffic.

"What the fuck does that mean?"

Kid smiles at me like I just got his meaning. Someone blares his horn at us since Kid's all over the place. Could be drunk, stoned, just a god-awful driver. But here's the thing. Much as he looked too young to have even a chance at being some fucked up version of Cave, I was beginning to wonder if it was possible. Maybe the way he lit his cigarette, picked at the edges of his nails, maybe it was when he leaned over and kissed me on the lips.

"Jesus fucking H!"

He licked his lips with his tongue. "I'm a bad seed."

"I don't care for men," I told him. "Boys neither."

He turned the radio on. Some old blues station. Old old blues. The sidewalk was whirring past, red lights too. I swear we hit a drunk. Bounced clean off the side of the blue sheet metal. Kid didn't even seem to notice. Had his arm around my shoulder now. "They call me Memphis Slim," he sang.

"Well Memphis," I said. "I'll be wanting to slide along now. I got myself a heavy-duty Friday night to take care of."

"S'fact?" He squeezed the ball of my shoulder. "What's the matter, don't you like my music?"

"It ain't pretty."

Kid laughed so loud. "What's your name, Riot?"

I saw an ambulance slip past my window, a gurney knocking at its back door.

"Well now not-so-pretty-boy, I am not sure that matters in any case."

Kid nodded. "That's about it," he said and cranked the music way up loud.

An hour later I'm still with him. We're cruising it seems. Up and down the lanes, windows down, music up. Some woman wailing about her daddy-beating-blues and Kid's lit another one up and he's beginning to look more like Nick Cave all the time. And while I have never been sweet on the Nickster his hand on my shoulder doesn't feel so heavy now, but we're still eyeing up the pretty girls, looking them over, up and down, in and out. Kid's undressing them I can tell and not just the pretty ones. Two buffed up beefcakes are going at one another with their feet and fists outside of some bar with a neon sign and a girl with a halter top, and the notice on the door doesn't say open or closed just "stop." But the buffed up ones don't, least not in my rear view mirror, and we're smelling blood in the Cadillac now, and it's still early and the Nickster seems not to notice. But he has altered, I can tell. He looks troubled. I half expect him to change the station on the radio. Instead, he removes his hand from my shoulder, lays it on my knee.

"You know what I am about to tell you?"

And how the fuck would I? But I say in any case, "I think I do."

Then he calls my bluff, and I don't know what to answer so I say, "You are about to tell me what a troubled soul you are."

And for a moment I think I might have hit it right, but then the coin spins and it drops. Kid laughs again. Squeezes my knee real tight, no friendship in it, plain badness, before rubbing it away. "Oh I'm that alright. But that's not it." He says it like I just lost a wager, like I owe him now. There's a crosswalk ahead with its lights flashing, but he doesn't stop, and he's looking at me as if he's waiting for me to pay up.

"I don't have anything," I tell him.

"I know that," he says.

The siren swirls around our ears like a whirlwind, a hurricane on the uptake, sucks us in to its vibrations. He pulls over to let the speeding truck past. "There are flames somewhere out of control."

I think of Mamie flopping about on my bed in the heat of the night, the rolling sweat beaded on her dark skin like mysterious fish eggs. And I think of her welcoming opened thighs. How she would grasp the hair at the scruff of my neck and pull tightly, how the mattress would creak and the light flicker, and the pain in my skin where she yanked and spoke garbled words. And that was before the other pain, the one that refused to yield. The one no amount of massaging by Kid's hand will ever ease.

"You got a girl stashed somewhere?' I ask him.

Kid looks bored by my question. "Guys like me, we got girls in every port. Every goddamned bar and backroom, open the John door they come tumbling out, one over another, tit over ass, got so many girls I couldn't give 'em all away if I tried."

I wasn't sure if I should weep for him or something. Kid like that.

It was going to rain, you could tell that. Kid would have to put the wipers on, and we'd watch them swishing across the glass, sweeping the water away like tears. Kid got me thinking that way, pathetic really.

"You don't believe me do you?" He was practically chewing on his cigarette.

"Why would I need to?"

"No reason. I just don't know why you wouldn't."

"No reason," I said.

"I didn't call you a liar."

"I didn't give you my name."

"Don't think I don't know who you are."

"I'm not saying you are a liar."

Kid moved his hand up off my knee along my thigh. "You can trust me."

"That's good to know," I told him. "It's not a common trait in this uncommon world."

What Kid could not have known is the trust I placed in Mamie, the same trust that fell astray, bounced off our pulsating bodies one hot and humid humping night and disappeared into the grinding dark. "Bless you," I said when we were done and Mamie's lusty lips pinched into prayer. Her twisted leg hobbled behind her as she left and her light dress clung to her pouting buttocks, and she turned in the doorway her black hair curling at her shoulders, and we just looked at one another, and there was no trust there anymore, her dress gathered at her waist, her bosom heaving in doubt, both of our bodies spent. Nothing. Nothing at all. And she just shook her head, and the eight years we had spent together spilled out on the wooden floor, and it was shameful to witness.

Back in the car Kid had suddenly started to cry. Like the rain I should have seen it coming.

"What's the matter?"

But Kid was blubbering too hard to respond even if he wanted to. And you had to believe it was a woman.

"Polly Jean?"

"What?" Kid stopped blubbering enough to reply.

"Polly Jean the problem?"

"Oh you're way off the mark," he said. "You're in a different time zone." He took his hand off my thigh and wiped his eyes. "Standing up there in the bright lights night after night you get to see things no one else sees," was what he said next. "It is so."

"Amen," I said.

"Brother, although I am not a man who believes in God I believe in Jesus."

"Amen," I repeated.

"They gather for you. They crowd the stage. Wait upon your every word, your every movement, your every breath."

"They're waiting for you to die."

"Fuck you."

"Trust me."

A woman stepped out from the kerb, all bangles and hair extensions, Kid too teared up to notice. I grabbed the wheel, steered him clear.

"What the fuck you do that for?"

"You could have killed her."

"Who?"

"Exactly."

"What the fuck you talking about?"

I pointed in the rear-view mirror. The woman stared after us, her hair streaming into the distance, her bangles jangling in shock.

Kid jammed the brakes. The tyres screeched to a stop. He looked hard into the mirror. Threw the car into reverse. "We're saved." He sped back where we had come from almost running her over for a second time. He pulled up beside her. She leaned in through the window all fucks and dickheads.

"Whoa lady, whoa," Kid crooned. "You're leaning through the wrong window for that." He pulled out his packet of cigarettes, offered one to her. "Go ahead. Go right ahead."

The woman drew her breath, ran her hand through her long extensions. "Nick Cave?"

Kid smiled. Pulled one of his cigarettes from the packet with his lips, offered one to her again.

"Oh my god. Nick Cave! Nick fucking Cave!" She took one.

Kid took a lighter from his pocket and lit both his and hers.

"I've been to your concerts."

"I've seen you there."

"You have? You saw me?"

"You would not believe the things I have seen. Come on, get in. We are holding up the traffic." And he was right. Horns were blaring, from all directions, everyone in the whole universe mad with us, desperately mad with us for coming to a halt in a time of movement.

The lady opened the rear door and got in. Kid stepped on the gas and we were back in the real world. Everything slipping past us faster than the eye could see. A red XXX neon sign flashed out its sporadic welcome and the first drops of rain splattered down upon us.

"God's plumbing is leaking," Kid said.

"My bath overflowed one time," the lady said. "Came down through the kitchen ceiling."

Kid tut-tutted.

"My Aunt Bella slid under when the taps were still running. Never did find out if she meant it or not."

The smoke from their cigarettes drifted through the Cadillac like polite condolences, stung my eyes. Maybe Mamie was somewhere out there on the streets just waiting to be seen with an accidental glance, a surprise turn of the head.

"She was like a mother to me."

"Understood."

"Raised me as though I was her own."

If I did see Mamie again, I would likely turn away. I do not think you can simply stop, reverse back and start all up again.

"I was only fourteen when the plaster in the ceiling cracked, when it all gave way."

"There's only so much you can mop up," Kid said.

"You understand me so well." The lady leaned in over the seat and stuck her tongue in Kid's ear, her arms around his neck.

Kid turned towards her and kissed her hard on the lips.

"The road, Nickster," I shouted.

He waved my shouts away. Her hand had found its way down to his groin, the hand with the cigarette still blazing. *I got the motherfuckingblue*s rasping in the air. Kid was on fire, the lady's tongue was steaming, the rain sizzled on the pent up glass, my heart hissed in my chest. We were on an invisible one-way lane and nothing now could stop us. Kid was practically clambering over the driver's seat, no one holding the wheel, and the lady's short skirt was shifting into high gear and as Kid fell between her moist and sweaty legs, the jangling of her bangles began in earnest, and I had no other option, like that time Mamie lost her mind beneath the heat of the glass houses in the tropical gardens, and I had no alternative but to quell her raving by striking her across the face with all my strength, and although she never quite forgave me I know I did no wrong, and so now with Kid and the lady rushing headlong in their own one-way lane I slid into the driver's seat and took the wheel and god forbid with the lady and Kid squealing hell for leather I turned the dial to something spruce and wholly innocuous, and with the push of a button the wipers wiped the rain away. That was when I saw the flashing lights of the police car and heard the sadness of its solitary siren.

"Kid," I shouted. "Kid, trouble."

But Kid was in another world. He and the lady were talking a language I couldn't understand.

"Gumbo, gumbo," I shouted back to no avail.

We could make a run for it, or we could make a stand. I saw the police officer step out of his car. So I drove up behind him and came to a halt. He approached my window. Kid and the lady were panting hard, but from where he was positioned he couldn't see them. Mamie had stood beneath a tall palm tree with a yellow and green parakeet flying behind her shoulder and screamed that she had larked in the park with her brother when they were only children who had known no better, and I knew that Mamie did not have a brother.

"Your name?" the policeman said.

"Nick Cave sir."

"Is this your vehicle?"

"Yes sir."

"You got a licence?"

"Yes, I do?"

"Can you take it out?"

I reached over the seat. Kid's ass was bopping up and down on top of lady, his mouth glued to hers like some weird form of psychosexual CPR. His pants hung down his legs. I stuck my hand in his back pocket and found his wallet. Took out his licence. Nicholas Edward fucking Cave. I handed it to the policeman. He looked at it, then looked at me.

"That doesn't look a bit like you," he said.

"I don't look a bit like me."

He stared at me a moment then handed it back. "Let me smell your breath."

He leaned into me, and I leaned in to him, our lips almost touching, and I breathed out deeply. I looked into his eyes. "You be on your way," he said. And I could smell his breath too. Coffee and peppermints, chicken salad sandwich, ballpoint pen, water-fountain water, fish chowder, right index fingernail, inner mouth flesh.

"I will." But I didn't move and neither did he. His tongue peeped out through his lips. "I know you."

"You might do," I told him.

"That doesn't give you any special rights."

"I know that."

"No you don't. You think it does. You think it puts you on top of some heap. Well I'm not a caretaker of heaps. You got the wrong springdingo here. I bet you're used to putting twenties where your mouth is, fifties even, hundreds. Isn't that so? Oiling the grinding wheels."

And it was then that Kid and the lady saw their destination come into view and were in an endless breathless hurry to reach it.

"What was that?" the policeman asked.

"Sir?"

Lady groaned... and Kid...

"What the?" The policeman broke our gaze, struggled to see in the back.

I reached into Kid's wallet again, pulled out two one-hundred-dollar notes, thrust them out through the window. The policeman looked at them dangling in my hand like used prophylactics. He grabbed them from me. "I'll be watching for you."

"I'll leave complementary tickets at the box office, that's a promise." And off I drove.

Lights changed to red and I stopped again. I didn't know this part of town well. Couldn't really say we were cruising anymore. Kid and the lady were smooching off their passion in the back. Lighting up cigarettes off one another, turning blind eyes to my heartlessness. The vehicles on green did their thing, straight ahead, left, right turns, wherever they were bound, cars, trucks, buses, their orange and red and yellow and white lights winking and twinkling as they departed. Two hipsters in a green station wagon gave me the finger. I was wishing I had Mamie with me up front whyever that would be. We were a thing of the past. A no-good thing of the past when it came to it. That time in the tropical greenhouse there were butterflies fluttering around like confetti, like we should have been getting married or something, and Mamie was screaming all those impossible incredible things that she believed were true, and the glass was stained in some sort of green powder and a dirty faded-pink flamingo limped behind a palm tree and the concrete floor was all damp and nothing smelled healthy and all I wanted was for Mamie to shut the fuck up, but she wouldn't, and this was a while before I was forced to slap her, and I could have put our eight years together in a box right then and snapped a lock shut on it and thrown it in the back of a dumpster and have walked clean away, I might never have looked back, and that's the goddamned truth, and this is the truth too, the dirty faded-pink flamingo stepped back out from behind the palm tree then and shit on the damp ground and who would have thought that flamingos shit but that's just what they do and what's more they don't give a shit. They shit right in front of you and they don't give a shit. And in the back of this blue Cadillac, Kid and the lady didn't give a shit either, one of the lady's tits hung right out of her blouse like that's where it belonged and the Nickster with his shirt end poking out of his fly like a flattened bleached dick, and me listening to whatever it is I am listening to on the radio, some easy listening trash, something that Nick Edward Cave would most probably despise more than Mamie despised me in the end. And she did despise me in the end. When she limped out of there with her dress clinging to her pouting buttocks there was hatred perspiring from her pores and who could blame her, and I did.

"We got ourselves a pair of green lights." Kid was back with me. Horns beeping impatiently from behind. I rolled on out of there.

Kid climbed over into the passenger seat, left the lady to her own devices. Tucked his white shirttail in and zipped his pants up. "You could most probably turn the wipers off."

They were screeching on the dry glass, the rain having long since stopped. One of the hipsters had a little wispy beard I would have liked to yank hard as I could, pull those tiny little hairs out one by one. I turned the wipers off, looked over at Kid.

"Nicholas Edward fucking Cave."

"The very same."

"It's a common enough name I guess."

The jangling lady asked to be let out.

I pulled over. She came around to Kid's window, leaned in and they kissed.

"Come see me again. I'm playing uptown next week."

She looked like she was about to draw away and then she stopped. "You saved my life on more than one occasion."

Kid looked pleased. "That's a sweet thing to say."

She kissed the tip of her index finger and laid it on his lips. I had enough at that point. I started the car up and pulled away abruptly, her hand and extended finger flew from his mouth out the open window.

The green station wagon turned out of the sidestreet to our right, two cars ahead of us. I followed after it. The car straight ahead took a left turn and we were down to one. A chicken shack soon filled the needs of the other vehicle and there we were. Us in the blue Cadillac and my fingering friends in the green station wagon.

I put my foot to the floor and swiftly kissed their ass. The station wagon jolted forward. Spun a half circle, and I was on it again. T-boning it. Shuffleboarding it down the street.

The front of the Cadillac was pretty riled up. One of the hipsters climbed out his window. The one with the wispy beard held his head in his hands. I put the Caddy in reverse, backed up a ways, did a sharp U-turn, took the first left turn I could and kept on going.

"What the fuck was that about?" Kid was asking.

"You hadn't had your head buried in that lady's wayward tits you might have known."

The street we were on now was deserted, barely lit.

"My fucking car!"

A black and white cat sprinted across the road. I saw the rainbow sheen of oil reflected off the one remaining light we had. And then I had a crazy thought. You would hardly credit it. Yes, I thought that maybe, just maybe that black and white cat was Mamie returning from the dead or wherever it was she had been hiding out in. And what I wanted to do was once again put my foot to the floor. I wanted to shoot forward as suddenly as a heartache and leave her as flattened as the Nickster's white shirt end and for what? Instead I drove through that puddle of rainbows and sprayed them every goddamn whichwhere. And then I stopped the car and told Kid to get the fuck out and he looked at me like I was crazy.

"Now lest you forget," he said, "this is my Cadillac, and you are my invited guest."

"That's not how I remember it," I told him. "Who's in the driving seat now?"

Kid breathed in slow and heavy, released it in the same way. "Lady told me you were trouble. And I told her that everyone was trouble, that that was nothing new, but she said that you were a special case. She said you were a particular brand of trouble, the kind that doesn't often meet the light of day. She told me I should stay away from you."

"Kid," I said, "her mouth was too busy back there to have let up for the length of time it would have taken to say all of that. Now you know all she told you was a bunch of grunts and hollers and groans."

"Isn't that what I'm telling you?" and Kid looked at me one more time like I really was the crazy one.

I don't want to go making too much of this, but it did occur to me later that my time in the blue Cadillac with Kid that black Friday night did resemble my time spent with Mamie right down to when I struck Kid in the face. And maybe that's the way of the world. Maybe we just keep doing the same things over and over again without making any significant changes and without learning a goddamned thing, and maybe all in all that is a good thing, who am I to say?

Mamie and I had plenty of good times together. "Think of it like a photo album," she said to me once, "there are some bad memories there, but then you turn the page, and there is a good one, and it helps you forget the bad one for a while." And surprisingly enough good memories don't take a lot was what she said. She never told me what happened to her leg, but I could guess, and I could probably guess wrong. Sometimes I pull out Kid's wallet, and I flash the driver's licence he had in there just like a photograph, Nicholas Edward Cave, and that's all it takes, and as I say, maybe that's enough.

"Don't forget," Kid said that night we parted rubbing his cut and swelling lip, "I know you."

And I like to think he did.

Salmon

Kevin Cahill

Chipper my uncle from Rocksavage called it,
tapping his toes with a tum-tit toe-tap,
joining two gitterns, a set of blubbing

musical bones, and one
salivating bagpipe. There we were
knee-deep in the Blackwater,

holding up a roe-rich
lump of smolt, soon to be poured
onto the oozy rocks of our palates.

Well, *his* palate. Attuned to the mouth-
watering purpose of the hunt,
he wrapped the victim up,

and carried it off. I was hardly out of short-pants,
but already I felt a chill current flowing
between me and the spirit of survival,

me and the breath of life. The salmon,
caught that day, was a barbed preamble
for things to come, for I stayed,

and stay still,
bone-dry on the bank,
clapping feebly to all this music.

THE WOMAN WHO USED TO BLEED
Lorraine McArdle

I was not born with a blackthorn sceptre cradled in my hand,
or a rook on my shoulder cawing incantations in my ear.

I have pricked my finger trying to push the eye of a needle through calico,
but no amount of stitches can stop holes opening in tunic folds,
or linen seams fraying at the edges where a rowan egg nestles in my breast.

I thought I would hear a sharp rap on the door, the toot of a bugle calling
time to drape soft pleats, this peachskin apron, around your waist.

Evening brings sloe berries that rise in my throat to burn my tongue with gin,
and dreams where I purge dozens of tiny peg dolls who once lived in my apron,
felt-tip smiles on wooden faces tell me I forgot to leave an ash leaf in the right shoe.

When I awake, I do not let the light from an Anglepoise lamp sting my eyes.
I open the curtains and watch a sickle moon carve platinum stars from vermeil gold.

A Tug in the Fall
Róisín Ryan

Well, I started to walk and on I went and it was coming on night when I got into the Ballyhoura
hills, that's better than ten miles from Kilmallock and there's a long lonely road after that. You
wouldn't see the sign of a Christian house along the road or hear a sound. It was pitch dark almost.
— Davin, *A Portrait of the Artist as a Young Man*

Ballyhoura country. Dark fertile valley
Spreading to where the Galtees lie on the
Land like naked, folded bodies, light-leached
And growing darker only. Landscape of
Unspoken rhythms, life lived by the
Mysteries of the earth. Landscape of lonely
Bachelors married to lonely girls. Light
Melts on the horizon. The valley is
Abandoned, the wooded Ballyhouras
Left to their nocturnal muttering. He
Doesn't know this place, doesn't know words like
Slievereagh, Seefin, Castlegale. He doesn't
Know that a man drove a pony and trap
Off that high bridge into empty fog, that
Those gaunt towers on that far hill saw
Many a man hanged, or so the whispers
Say. Mountain trees stand like the skeletons
Of giants. The undergrowth turns black, thickens.
Glowing eyes float in the rustle. Bats jag
The air, unseen water quickens. The white
Of a barn owl spreads on the dark, like an
Omen.
   Up ahead, at the curve of the
Track, a cottage hoards warm light against the
Dark. Its white walls glow blue in the night. He
Knocks, she opens the door like she knew he
Was coming. He explains, his throat is parched,
He is on a long journey. She obliges
Him with a mug of milk. Her hair falls darkly
Around her face. Something about the dark
Softness of her eyes, a tug in the fall

Of her long shift suggests a baby, maybe
Sometime before May. Landscape of lonely
Bachelors married to lonely girls. Her
Husband is far away, gone to see a
Sister to the boat. Her mouth says don't be
Afraid. Her eyes threaten to swallow him
Whole. The Ballyhoura darkness presses
Closer. He grips the mug like a prison
Bar, he wishes he had never come. Her
Thin fingers take his fingers, his hand. The
Flickering light makes her head a skull. He
Cannot stay, for more reasons than one. He
Steps back into the night, cool against his
Addled blood. He has promises to think
Of, a mother who would ask. He leaves her
Face burning like a spirit in the dark.
She leaves nothing but a mark on the
Memory, dark and troubling as candlewax.

PHOTO ESSAY
John Minihan

Mark Doty, 2012

Douglas Dunn, 2015

Victoria Kennefick, 2015

James Harpur, 2015

Paisley Rekdal , 2016

Matthew Dickman, 2017

Karen Solie, 2017

Nuala Ní Dhomhnaill, 2017

Thomas McCarthy, 2017

Maram al-Masri, 2017

Yusef Komunyakaa, Carolyn Forché, Theo Dorgan, Paula Meehan, 2017

Aleš Šteger, 2018

RYAN'S YELLOW AND BLUE BRAIN
Jose Varghese

Ryan's friends have typical South Indian names, but his parents do everything different. He doesn't understand why they do things their way when it's less troublesome to do what everyone else does. His friends have got used to the name but they won't miss an opportunity to tease him when the teachers pronounce 'Ryan' in various wrong ways, sometimes with a scoff so evident that his face goes pink, then red, with shame and anger. That's when he feels that the whole world is against him, with not a soul to care for his feelings.

He has stopped complaining to his mother about the name. It's hard to talk with her about anything, not to mention those topics that he needs to talk about. And he doesn't enjoy talking with anyone at all these days, because none of them give him the space to do that on his terms. Mother says he has to focus only on what's necessary for a schoolkid to survive on this planet.

'Take your mind off of those hundreds of other things, Ryan', she says. 'Oh Jesus! These are like a curse... or are they someone's black magic, leading this boy to silly visions, one after the other, fascinating and distracting him?'

And so her rant would go, and Ryan would make a quiet exit and walk towards his secret spot below the nearby hillock where he can sit all alone and listen to the rivulet hurrying forward and watch kingfishers swishing past him or perched on their secret branches keeping a furtive eye on the fish below. There are other birds and little animals that he thinks are constantly seeking his attention through their unexpected moves or calls, trying to tell him something in a language that he doesn't understand.

Mother hates his recent obsession with horrible deaths, be it from real life or from his silly dreams. She complains that the red flag that his father worships has drowned Ryan's good sense in those blood-filled images. What else is needed to ruin a perfect childhood! He's no more the god-fearing boy she had raised him to be.

Ryan's dreams about death involve gruesome details. He doesn't enjoy any of them in particular, but he's so used to them that his sleep seems incomplete in their absence.

A teacher said recently that we'll remember even the minute details from our dreams if we stay in bed for a few extra minutes after waking up, but that's possible for him only on weekends. That's when he would manage to stay a little longer in his bed, pretending to be still asleep, and try to recount all those visions that unfurl in a manner similar to colourful cartoons. He doesn't like to visualize anyone getting hurt, and the dreams don't really involve any of that, but what he sees are unsettling in other ways. As mother says, they fascinate and distract him at the same time. He knows about their origins, but he is clueless when it comes to making sense of the curious combinations in which they present themselves to him. He would try hard to find hidden clues, as if they were a puzzle that he had to solve. Sometimes he would look for details the same way he does during his art lessons at school.

The images are of limbs severed, innards lying around, blood flowing in streams and transforming the gutters on his village roads to pools big enough for a toddler to swim in. But they aren't scary to him because the colour schemes are different from what they must be in reality, and the objects he often associates with them are not of the blood-curdling type. He likes to see what our bodies are made of, and he has seen those anatomy diagrams and sculptures, and even a human skeleton in a glass cage, in the little science lab at school. He wonders why people look at the same things differently in different contexts. He would stare at the mysterious ways in which bones and intestines and stomachs and windpipes and muscles and nerves and skin intermingle and transform from one thing to the other, as his dreams guide him to extend reality to new dimensions. Good if he can have a vision of a skull breaking open magically, like a tender coconut shell and the brain spilling out in golden light, half in and half out, half solid and half fluid, half yellow and half blue, which he thinks all brains are. He sees more of these images if he'd listened too long to the people in his village who revel in the macabre and love describing abnormal deaths for months on. It's hard to stay away from them these days, as there's a lot of time that he has to spend all by himself after school, till his mother finishes the household chores and waits for father to come home. Ryan runs errands and gets stuck with the stories that involve drama, gossip and horror, told in seemingly authentic voices by those people who hang around in the small marketplace to while away their time.

His art teacher had once stopped his father in the street and told him that he's a talented kid who needs special attention, and that it might be a good idea to send him to art college when he grows up. But that will take around ten more years, father said, to think of choosing a college.

'He told me that your mind is like a sponge', father said. 'He also thinks you lack original visions at the moment, as you are always engaged with absorbing and copying things instead, from what you see around you. But that's all right, he says, because you're only seven now.'

Would it be the same if he absorbed and copied from what he saw in his dreams? He wasn't sure that anyone would love to see those disturbing images as art. Would it be a good idea if he tries to draw them once, at least for himself? But who cares?

Today he'd lost his cool in the morning because he came to know, first thing on such a fine Saturday, that his parents don't care two straws for the first ever major demand that he has made on his birthday. He hasn't asked for something they can't afford. All that he needs is a bicycle. Father said in clear terms that it's not the 'need of the hour', just before hurrying out for work. Mother avoids the subject altogether. She pretends she's more concerned about his dream visions when he tries to speak to her. She had been prompting him to pray every day to get rid of them, and Ryan doesn't actually have anything against prayers. He loves the hymns he sings with mother for the night prayers. He loves the portrait of Jesus in their portico, especially those light brown eyes that remind him of the eyes of the deer he saw during a school trip to the local zoo. He thinks Jesus has more in common with such animals than humans, by the way he looks and conducts himself. Mother doesn't get that at all. For her, Jesus is above all humans, and everything else, in the living and nonliving world.

'Stop watching these silly animals and thinking too much about them,' she says.

His father would escape to his room each day before they start the prayers. He keeps saying that 24 hours a day aren't enough for him to run his driving school and to remain a political animal, helping the poor and the dispossessed.

'We can't afford to indulge in futile rituals and superstitious customs,' he would say. 'That's a lazy bourgeoisie luxury.'

Ryan doesn't understand what that implies, but likes the smooth flow of these words. The only thing he admires about his father is the way he speaks, using big words that he seldom understands. There's something about the voice too, as if what's said is not meant for one or two individuals but a crowd, and not for one occasion, but for the times to come. Ryan hopes he will be able to speak like that, some day.

The last he sees of father each day is at the dinner table. That's when his breath smells of alcohol and onions.

'It won't harm anyone if you say grace before you eat', mother would say.

'No grace in having a full meal when millions starve elsewhere!'

Father would never fail to say something to that effect each day, winking at Ryan. That would be enough to make mother feel left out. She would end up doing the dishes noisily, lamenting that it's blasphemy she gets in return for a good attempt to talk.

Ryan used to be proud of his father's Mark II Ambassador car when he was younger. His friends have now nicknamed it 'Limping Amby' though it's still capable of moving swiftly through the village roads. It's light green, and he loves that colour because it reminds him of parakeets. He used to press his cheek against its body to feel how cold the metal was. It had a pleasant smell, like his mother's nail polish that she would wear on

Mondays and remove on Sundays before going to church. There used to be a time when he loved sitting snuggled with her in the back seat of the car, or on other occasions, in the front seat next to his father. He enjoyed the murmur of the wind rubbing past his cheeks as he struggled to keep his eyes open to see the trees and small buildings moving past. Everyone had enough time for everyone else those days. He even felt the car was like a member of their family, though he didn't really like it when father gave some extra attention to it on certain days when it needed some repair. It was cool to own a car in a village where people had no choice other than to wait in the morning or evening for the two state transport buses if they wanted to go to the nearby town. But now Mark IV rules the 1980s Indian roads, and Ryan is seven years old. Old enough to tell the difference.

It will come soon, rattling on its way downhill, passing the narrow winding road after the bridge. Ryan had been sitting for too long on a large rock that's at an equal distance, two furlongs perhaps, between the marketplace and home. He had been moving from one thing to another like a machine the whole morning and afternoon, with his thoughts revolving around the bicycle. Now he knows what he should do, as the time of his father's return is getting close. His heart keeps thumping against his ribs. Both sides of the road are covered in thick foliage. Quite often, an alarmed mongoose would run across the road when a car or motorbike passed by, and escape narrowly. On those occasions when his father took Ryan and mother to the Talkies in the town for matinees and to return late in the evening, it would shock his mother each time a mongoose flitted across. His father would slow down the car a bit and chuckle.

'Look how crazy these animals are! They're tempting fate when they don't have to.'

'God Almighty guards them! Don't be too sure about what each living things mean in His eyes,' mother would say.

'Oh come on, don't drag your God Almighty to this!' father would say. 'He, or She, is too busy to watch over all the mongooses in the world. You make it sound like guarding these little creatures from their own mischief is top priority out there!'

Father would then drown the scope for further conversation in the loud whistling of one of his favourite Hindi songs. Mother didn't really mind that those days, because she liked father's singing, though she kept saying that his Hindi pronunciation was horrible. It's been ages since Ryan spent such good time with them, or even heard him singing. Now, he shouldn't give father any time to apply the brake. He must move like a shooting star, much faster than the mongoose. There's actually no space to swerve the car to the right because of the big trees, and the thick bushes on the left would rule out the other option as well; unless his father is foolish enough to ride over them to let the car tumble to the canal twenty foot down. No, he isn't foolish. He won't let anything happen to his stupid limping Amby, or to his own life.

Life is already hard enough for Ryan. It's the same for his best friends in school, Vijay and Priya. Vijay sits next to him on the same bench, and Priya sits on the adjacent bench that's meant only for girls. Ryan used to draw their portraits on his slate when the teacher wasn't looking in their direction. They would look at the portraits which were more like negative images, with the gray pencil strokes on the black slate, and talk about their weekend plans, though there weren't really any plans except for accompanying parents when they went for a wedding reception or a funeral. But even those days filled with simple and silly moments spent in friendly talk are gone now.

Vijay's father hanged himself from a mango tree next to their house. People say that it's because Vijay's beautiful mother had an affair with someone smarter than his stupid father. They make it a point that Vijay hears each word of what they say. The ripe mangoes from that tree, for which school kids would fight all the time, lie unwanted on the ground these days. The numerous squirrels on the tree don't care for the fallen mangoes, as there are still a lot of ripe mangoes hanging from the branches. They love to jump on the mangoes in what looks like a suicidal act. But they never miss their aim and hug the mangoes as if they were their lovers and sway with them in the air for a while before feeling their skin, taking in their scent, kissing, and then nibbling on them obsessively, tails moving this way and that. Ants, flies, and worms get on the mangoes lying on the ground, and then leave them to rot. Ryan envies these little animals and insects for their careless acts of moving from one thing to the other without bothering much about what the world thinks about them.

Priya's eyes are always bloodshot nowadays. It seems she's taken up crying as a full-time occupation at home. Her habit of rubbing and squeezing her eyes makes them look redder and darker. Her mother drank acid and had a death as miserable as her life. Ryan heard vivid descriptions of how acid can burn your throat and intestines. He knows that everyone in the village makes sure that Priya hears all of these descriptions too. Her father drinks more after the incident and beats up Priya, because he can't beat up her mother anymore. Only God knows what awaits her, as days, weeks, and months pass by, making her eyes redder and body leaner.

Ryan feels friendless with his two dear friends silenced. The science teacher even mentioned one day that these kids must be going through what is described in the Holy Books as hell. Ryan doesn't find any sense in that, as the real sinners are not his friends. The sinners are already dead and gone or alive and sinning more. He doesn't trouble Vijay and Priya though, because he doesn't want his words or actions to add more to their suffering. The people in the village never forgive the dead, and the living.

'But these are poor people', Ryan's mother keeps saying. 'All they have to lose are their worthless lives. If they had something valuable in life, they wouldn't do such foolish things.'

'Are we rich then?' Ryan would ask.

'Not really. We are middle class, to the lower side of it. Higher middle class and rich people have better cars for themselves.'

Ryan's father's school is his car. He teaches all the rich and middle-class men in the village to drive, and to get licenses. The poor have no choice. If they had enough money to pay the fees for driving lessons, they would rather eat three times a day for a whole month.

The rich would eventually buy their own cars and drive them all around, showing it off as a 'status symbol'. The lower middle-class men aspire to become taxi drivers and make a living out of it. Some among them dream of working as drivers of taxis or trucks in what they call the Gulf countries. A few women from the nearby town join the school too because they want to drive their own cars when they move to the USA or Europe, to work as doctors or nurses, or to become the wives of doctors or nurses.

'It's the hardest job on earth to teach smart people how to drive a car', his father would say. 'It's much easier if they are stupid and their brains are wired simpler. The doctors and teachers, you see, they have it all messed up with heavy information packed too tight in their brains that it's impossible to receive simple instructions or to do easy tasks.'

But he doesn't teach Ryan, his only son, how to drive a car. His brain is all yellow and blue, wired simple, fresh to receive instructions. Father doesn't even allow Ryan to touch the steering wheel or play with the knobs and buttons on the dashboard. The only luxury he has as the son of a car owner is the occasional opportunity to help his father wash the car.

Well, his father says that he has to be eighteen years old to get a license to drive.

'It's not about learning how to maneuver the car. Anyone might learn it with a lot of practice. It's really about taking a decision in a fraction of a second. Machines just obey your decisions. They can't judge what's more valuable, what's to be saved, when you're left with a difficult choice.'

But what are the flimsy excuses he has for not buying a bicycle for Ryan? He doesn't need to worry too much about choices with a bicycle. It doesn't really kill anyone. He hasn't at least heard of horrible deaths that involved a bicycle.

Father says that there isn't enough money. That Ryan is not old enough. That none of his friends in school have it.

But his friends aren't like him. They are poor!

Rich kids go to another school. It's four or five times bigger than Ryan's, and no one who doesn't study or work there can get inside the high walls surrounding it. Ryan's school is a lame affair – an L-shaped building with eight classrooms and a staff room, a line of hibiscus plants in the courtyard, a well in the corner, and a shabby shed where rice porridge and a mung bean dish is prepared on school days, as free lunch for all the students. But he has heard that the rich kids' school has all kinds of food that they can buy, a small zoo, tall trees and flowering plants in a park, a fountain, separate playgrounds and courts for tennis, cricket, football and basketball, and wonder of wonders, a swimming pool.

And all those kids own colourful bicycles. They ride them proudly. As they pass through the street, a pleasant fragrance from their uniforms spreads all around. They look so new, the uniforms, as if they are just taken off the shelves of a textile shop. Ryan and his friends would inhale those fragrances as these kids passed by on their bicycles. He would wonder whether the fragrance came from the detergent soaps used to wash their clothes, or from the scents in bottles that people in big cities apply on their bodies and clothes to cover up their bad smells, or simply from the happiness of owning such beautiful bikes.

Ryan doesn't really want to go to the rich kids' school because he heard that they teach all the subjects in English there. The kids speak in English to one another, and would ignore Ryan and his friends when they called out to them in Malayalam. Priya would say that the boys are much taller than Ryan and Vijay, so it's better not to offend them. Vijay would say that they are big show-offs, pretending that they don't understand their own language. English doesn't sound good to Ryan, anyway. He doesn't understand any of it. Life is already too complicated. Why add more complication with a language that he doesn't even like? But he fancies those bicycles.

Father says that he has to wait. Ryan knows that he is being fooled. Mother fights with father every night because he drinks and distributes all his money to people with 'greater needs'. He doesn't beat up mother like the other husbands in the village, but she would say he wastes all the money that he owes his family to his charity and alcohol. He would shout at her for a while, and then just sit staring at her as she loses her calm and outshouts him. Mother would end up weeping and saying that her life is a lost cause, trapped in a home that's dominated by a crazy idealistic man and a senseless mischief of a son, with no other female around to understand her, to talk or fight with, the way she likes it.

Ryan doesn't talk about the bicycle to his mother. He knows that it's useless. She has no money, and no influence over his father, despite all that lung power and shouting skills. And his father says that he has no money for a bike, for his only son, on his birthday. Death will teach him a lesson.

Ryan hears the rickety sound as a car moves over the bridge. He can in fact trace the light-green colour and the driving school label of his father's Amby, as it winds down the path to the bridge. To make sure, he looks for the L sign. Yes. As the car moves down the road, he can even catch a glimpse of his father's salt-and-pepper beard and the cream-and-blue checked shirt he wears most days. There's just enough time. The car speeds up as it comes closer. His heart pumps against his ribs.

He considers life without a bicycle. It's bad, beyond doubt. There's nothing else to make him happy in it. He shuts his eyes tight and jumps as far as he can, faster than the mongoose, to the middle of the road. Did he reach far enough?

A screech and a thud.

Nothing hits him, but something passes behind him at great speed like a hurricane. Twigs break. Does a tree branch fall down on metal? Does his father scream? Ryan lies on his stomach on the road, afraid to open his eyes. He senses an unpleasant pain around the right knee. He hears his father open the door and walk towards him on unsteady feet, crushing the grass under his sandals, and now, his breath can be heard right above his head.

Father's hands move in a rough manner as they turn him over and go under his back to lift him up, though the roughness melts mid-way. He is drawn slowly towards father's chest. He opens his eyes to see father crying, breathing heavily. Tears roll down his face, falling to Ryan's forehead. Their bodies shake.

'Why did you do this, dumb boy?' father mutters.

Ryan looks around for the car, and sees it stuck against a tree on the right. One of its rearview mirrors is broken and a corner of its sturdy bonnet is crushed by a branch that has fallen on it. The boot of the car is slightly open, and he sees, gleaming through that gap, a brand-new bike with blue metal bars, secured safe with yellow plastic rope. There's a box next to it, with colourful images of art supplies.

He feels his heart in his throat. He wants to tell father that he wants to die, that he doesn't want to listen to him and mother fighting all the time, that he wants to be reborn in a better place, as a rich boy who can get a bike without a fight. That it wasn't the bike that really mattered. That he wanted them to stop fighting and to listen to him, their only son, at least on his birthday. That he hates the smell of alcohol and onions.

But father's crying doesn't allow Ryan to say any of it. He could have kicked himself free from father's grasp if he were angry or beating him. He could have run away to some distance and stood firmly on the ground, looked him in the eye, man to man, and shouted all these, and more.

But now he is carried towards the car, as father keeps crying, speaking gibberish, and calls him 'my child, my only child, little idiot, dunce', and so on.

Ryan realizes that there is no smell of alcohol and onions today. A strange kind of silence surrounds him and he starts hearing, with his ears pressed to his father's chest, the weary heartbeat going too fast on an unsteady rhythm.

Then he begins to see the scene from high above as if he was an eagle circling around, looking for clues and details that it has to bring together to make sense of its life in a moment before it descends to the mundane affair of zeroing in on possible prey that present before its eyes. The varying shades of greens and yellows and ochres and blues float below him, inviting him to make them a part of his breath and to allow them to be the mysterious elements of his cells. He realizes how he's part of the vast canvas and begins to understand his folly of trying to alter the balance of life in a moment of revolt and how the forces around them are keeping an eye on these two helpless people who carry their grief and regret and relief and hope to the car that's waiting patiently for them. Now that they remain protected and unharmed, they have to repair themselves and bring back their world to its original state of innocence.

Everything blurs then, and he hugs father tight. It seems like more than seventeen long years since he had last hugged his father, though he is only seven now. That's what his yellow and blue brain feels.

ZUNDERT

Tomás de Faoite

I

I get work in a vegetable processing factory
in Zundert, the birth place of van Gogh,
eight hours a day separating big cucumber
from small, on a production line that goes on
until I'm the one who is moving and the con-
veyor belt is still. After eight hours of pure
drudgery, mind-numbing work, the sky
for one brief moment is cucumber green
when I come out, like northern lights seen
in daylight hours. Then I return home by
bus through a landscape of young trees
of evergreen sapling, so still and so soft
like lushrooms of the earth, their heads
barely visible thirty nine feet above the sea.

II

Van the man Gogh, man Gogh…
Crows in your head, darkening
the picture. Although mad with colour
for years a bit of black is called for.
Caw-caw said a crow to another crow
who cawed back. Why? Be caws.
So why did van Gogh shoot himself,
cut his ear off? Not even his brother
Theo knew why. Then years later
his distant cousin Theo is stabbed
in the street in Amsterdam, because
he had said too much whereas
Vincent had heard too much,
cinder songs in crows' throats.

MISSING

Daragh Byrne

A spate of garden gnomes that summer,
our village colonised overnight—

their crimson caps and foolish little boots
suddenly ubiquitous. Gnomes on the bridge

directing traffic, gnomes hosting tea parties
on occupied lawns, gnomes smoking cigarettes

by the riverbank. A kayaker pursued one
paddling off in his kayak. An amateur astronomer

photographed gnomic shadows on the moon.
A farmer swore he witnessed

a coven of the little fuckers treading circles
in his crops, but nobody believed farmers

in the village. My instinct was to blame you—
that stunt with the cockatoos

in the church eaves last year; the spectacle
of the Swiss cheeses with their holes

filled in—nobody could prove anything,
but I knew it was you, brother.

You'd skipped town two days before
the visitors arrived—the village

emptied of you, as if in preparation.
Later in the week, the police estimated that

gnomes now accounted for twenty-eight percent
of the biomass of the parish;

there was talk in the cafés of land rights
and barricades. The police also said that,

in most cases, missing persons turn up
within two weeks. The gnomes

disappeared shortly after. I still hope
that you will come back.

THE PLAY

Jane Robinson

to Matthew Sweeney

I'll make you a character
in my next play where a visitor
to the falling ice hotel, melting
crystals everywhere sliding
the carpet from underfoot,
meets an enormous woman
dressed in a fish tail –
the Mermaid of the North
or Steller's sea cow,
now extinct – and discusses
with her the meaning of life
and other important matters
while sipping *uisce beatha.*

I met you once, but was too shy
to say anything at all. I'm sorry
now. Having slept curled
like a cat at the feet of my father
on his last night, I should have
seen how short the time.
I could have given you a grin,
said something encouraging
or wise – instead I'm left
catching a bus to Donegal
with my beautiful daughter
to film your last screenplay,
the one with the grave.

13 WAYS OF LOOKING AT A GHOST
Róisín Leggett Bohan

after W.S.

I
Through the wisps of smoke rings that halo a tipsy mouse,
I see a ghost serenading the night sky with shadow mist

II
Where there is one ghost, there is always more than one ghost,
perching on the treacherous lap of summer

III
Acrobatic crows sip dew through thin lips and spit sibilant sentences;
they fall like waterfalls, soothe the tired feet of ghosts

IV
If you meet the nippy desert fox on the puritanical bus,
I would suggest – *go sit at the back* with the smoking ghost

V
The song of ghosts can be tracked by jaguars from 78 miles away
Some say it is tequila that heightens their senses

VI
The onomatopoeic ferret chews the fingernails of nervous ghosts
who get extra pointy but lose their sense of direction

VII
Ghosts eat crimson horse hooves for second breakfast
Stumbling inebriated clouds call – *ugh!*

VIII
What if the milk-soaked peat sucked deep on the marrow of earthworms?
Would more ghosts grow?

IX

Ghosts lick the dizzy howls of wolves
On misshapen nights, owls record their movements

X

Drowsy cigarette ends shed their amber husks
to weave tobacco huts for the ghosts of shrews

XI

The waistcoated ant drives his campervan through the night forest
He signals with a V sign when he comes across dancing ghosts

XII

The lonely squirrel poaches the sick rain that trickles
down the manes of the galloping ghosts of horses

XIII

And what of the sexy sparrow who hops on and off her fizzy blue fern?
Does she see ghost sparrows playing strip poker on the eagle soaring over Guadalquivir?

MOON
Geraldine Mitchell

How is it that this cold, this lost and lonely
mirror ball, this fickle silver coin minted in
the sun's fierce heat, this senseless object of
age-old adoration, can come robbing sleep
when she's already full and should need for

nothing more? A shaft of silent light has startled me
awake, her hands are round my neck, her silky fingers
slipping from the cut glass bauble there to trap
the evening sun and set it splintering. Moon's
rainbow shards are faint as rain. I step into

the pewtered garden under a rash of stars,
hear night sounds of sleeping trees, lay
a finger on my pulse, begin to measure
loss in years, love in generations.
I have become my own blanched ghost.

ON HOLD
Patrick Holloway

Paul had a way of taking what he wanted.

'Oh, if nobody wants this then, I suppose I'll take it,' he said as we first started to go through our parents' bills, debts, letters. I turned to see it was a painted wooden hen that had little hooks to hang their keys. Another random object my mother had probably picked up in a charity shop. No keys, I thought, to hang any longer. And without objection from the five of us he left the room and went down the hall and I heard him rummaging in our parents' bedroom.

We sat around the table on which I had studied for the Junior and Leaving Cert. This house though had never really been ours; none of us had lived there. My parents had downsized a few years after we had all moved out, relocating to the back fields of Minane Bridge, to a bungalow with a view of cascading greens. The last time I was home, my father had said he enjoyed seeing tractors in the distance, like specks, like little wings of shadow among the fields. Busying their way up and down and up again. It's really quite peaceful, he said, a lovely place to bring up children, looking at me, judging, as if by not giving birth I had already failed in life. I probably answered with something like, I bet it is, look I'm just going out to meet the girls… and gave some wilting excuse, using words that were far away from him, that had a meaning but not one he could place.

My brothers and sister and I sat around trying to talk. Being the fifth child, the forgotten, flaky one, I waited for Francis to take control, even though Maggie was more prepared, and the eldest. I had seen Maggie in action many times, in a courthouse, in a bar, a fierce fight in her, but at home she curtailed, making tea and serving milk, asking if anyone wanted more biscuits. All the London must have leaked out of her on the way back over.

'Well, the will is clear, fairly clear anyway,' Francis started. He always did that, repeated parts of phrases. *It's a beautiful day, a really beautiful day. I got the call, I was the first to get the call.* Looking at him now, his forehead already that of a man just past middle age, with a cross on show beneath the open buttons of his shirt, I thought him very provincial. I did not want to feel pity for him, for any of them really, nor did I want to be dragged back into the intricacies of what love meant among siblings, of what was expected of me, just because I was a sister; a daughter no more. I wanted to be there for as little time as possible.

'I'm having a colleague look over it,' said Maggie. 'I don't want to be the one executing it; it's better to be impartial.'

'First thing, I suppose, is to know what to do with the house, easiest thing would be to sell it and split the money between us.' Francis again, looking round at all of us, catching my eye so I looked away and saw Timmy with his head down, wiping at his eyes with his sleeve. He looked up at me and I smiled. Poor old timid Timmy, the youngest but not always so. The only one I could truly say I loved— distinctive, dug-deep love. He lived in Carrigaline and had visited them almost daily. Practically moved in with mum when dad passed away. He was the one who had brought the shopping each day, who had helped them use Zoom, who visited dad in hospital at the end; he was the one who found mum at home just a few weeks ago, stiff. Like one of those wax statues, he'd told me, that's what she was like, lying there in the bed.

I hadn't made it back for either of the funerals and it suited me well enough. Australia was far; my job demanding. Maggie had told me if I'd really wanted to, I could have made it, she had after all. Stephen said the same. He lived in Fontainebleau, just outside Paris. He had owned a chain of English language schools and sold them only a few years ago and could now afford to live just writing opinion pieces and non-fiction for not much money at all. He didn't need it. He was already moneyed. Stephen was the most handsome, kept himself in shape and wore a Rolex. He loved to answer calls, especially when he got to speak his languid French. He'd turn to make sure those nearby were impressed. In the silence after Francis spoke, Stephen was the first to talk.

'I'm easy,' he said, 'whatever ye decide to do is fine by me.' He looked around and caught my eye. Whichever way he smiled he reminded me of our father. A pang of anger surfaced. My father hadn't taken his cancer seriously, being pious he thought he was immune to suffering, to repent; everything was god's will, the lord have mercy and all the imbecilic bullshit he came out with. My mother, a shadow of the midday sun, nodded and said yes, things will be fine, what will be will be. Doris Day was her religion. She spent her weekends at the dog shelter near North Main Street.

'I mean unless someone wants to stay with the house. If someone wanted to keep the house, then it would complicate things.'

We all looked at Timmy. He was the only one who still lived in Cork; the other two who had stayed in Ireland were Francis—living in Galway, and Paul—living in Dublin. Francis wouldn't want the house for he was happy out as a principal in Salthill and, like my father, a church goer, helper, giver. A fool. Paul probably didn't want the house either, just everything in it, he'd probably already nabbed loose earrings and cuff links, things that he could sell to little jewellers or at auctions or online. I could see a woman exactly like my mother picking up my mother's earrings for 15 euro. A steal, she'd call them, showing them off to friends. I missed her then, terribly, abruptly.

I got up from the table to go to the toilet. I heard Francis sigh and talk to Stephen.

They were quiet enough so I couldn't draw attention to it as I reached the door. If I had they would have said it was nothing, that I was being sensitive again, not everything was about me. So I walked out of the kitchen and saw the large statue of the Virgin Mary by the front door. It was even too big for our childhood home but in a two-bedroom bungalow it looked ridiculous.

The downstairs toilet was cluttered. The whole place was cluttered. My mother's limited allowance all spent on trinkets and cheap wooden objects with carved words. Every cloud has a silver lining was written below a mirror, in the shape of a cloud. My poor mother, she thought those things motivating, she must have thought that people who stood there looking at themselves would admire it, that it would make them think, yes, yes, every cloud does, I should be more positive, well, that was an easy fix.

I always looked different when I was around them. My face longer, somehow; terse, skin stretched to fit jutting cheekbones and a pointy chin. Behind me, reflected, was the shower, the long-slanted handrail to help them in and out. I saw them so seldom that their ageing always jolted me. The longer I was away, the easier it became. When I would visit, though, the time between us stretched and tightened so everything around us was at odd angles.

There was a gap of eight years between Paul and myself, so it went like this: Maggie, Francis, Stephen and Paul were one set of siblings; then me, Timmy and Anthony another. My mother spent nine years being pregnant, having miscarriages, and giving birth. It's why, I think, when Anthony was born and the doctors told her there'd been some slight complications in the birth and that she wouldn't be having any more babies, she looked upon Anthony as the only miracle among us.

I was hoping for a baby sister and cried when I was told it was another boy. Then when they came home from the hospital and I saw him all swaddled in stitched blues, I cried again, for he was the most beautiful little thing I'd ever seen. He became our toy, Timmy's and mine. I was five and Timmy was three and Anthony was brand new. I always wanted to be next to him. I watched as my mother breastfed him, how he suckled, his little fists all movement. It's then I started to love my mother, for before that she was just a strict presence, scolding me in between scolding the others. I thought there was no love in her at all and then Anthony was born and I got to bathe in their love.

Back in the kitchen Francis and Stephen were talking. Paul had found his way back in and was listening intently to their views about how things would be split among us as I sat back down.

'Anyone for more tea?' Maggie said, moving past the island and to the fridge.

'Is there any beer or wine or something?' I asked.

'Jesus Kate, it's only a quarter to eleven,' Francis again, the look of horror on his face as he tapped his simple, non-Rolex watch in front of me. Those poor students of his poor school.

'There's a bottle of Chardonnay,' Maggie said, 'I might join you.'

She came back to the table with the bottle and four glasses. I took one, as did she, and Timmy and Paul. It had been decided that the house would be sold. I stretched my arm out under the table and squeezed Timmy's knee. You ok? I mouthed, and he barely nodded.

'Well, getting back to it, if we may,' Francis gave me a doctrinal look, 'there is just so much stuff here, really, just so much of it, we have to decide who wants what, really. I mean the beds, couches, bigger stuff, I think we could try and sell, or, if it were up to me, we could donate to one of the local charities. I know the Carrigaline church helps with things like this.'

'The church has taken enough from us,' I said and stared at Francis. He looked at me as if I were a stain on cloth that just wouldn't come out.

'Then what is it you suppose, Kate, what is it that you suppose we do in a situation like this?'

'Honestly, I couldn't give the wildest, as long as the church stays out of it.'

'I agree.' Maggie said, 'I think after all that's happened it's better to just keep everything between the six of us. Let's decide that way.'

'I think,' I started again, now I knew Maggie was on my side, 'that Timmy should get to choose if he wants anything. To be fair like, he's the only one who still lives here and was the one who took care of them.'

He didn't look up, always nervous when he was the subject of the conversation. Maggie nodded in agreement, as did Stephen. Francis stayed quiet and Paul scoffed. The conversation kind of went stale and a little pause came, then Stephen started asking Maggie about the situation in London. Paul had slithered over to Francis. Timmy looked up at me and I nodded towards the back door to the garden, picked up my wine glass and left. He followed and we sat outside sipping wine.

I had grown up with Timmy's silence and had seen people rummage around for words to fill it, had felt their stickiness as they forced smiles and looked for someone else to jump in. He was the only person I could sit in silence with, it was soft and welcoming, like a fire lit and burning on a cold Sunday after morning mass. We weren't that religious. Just my father, who had gone to mass every day with his father. The rest of us were a normal family, going two Sundays a month, ticking the boxes that pass for a Catholic in a rural Irish village.

One morning we were playing, Timmy, Anthony and I. Out in the back garden. Anthony was four, Timmy six, and I had just turned eight. It was Saturday or Sunday, I don't remember, and dad was heading out. He came around the side of the house and said he'd be back shortly and to be good and not drive my mother up the walls. I ran down and hugged him, then Timmy did the same. My father was in a rush, kind of only half hugging us and then striding away. Anthony hadn't noticed us running down and my father didn't wait for Anthony to catch up. I never knew why but it was obvious my father never really loved Anthony. I'd think it over for years and years and the closest I could come to a reason was that he was told he could not have any more kids after Anthony. I can't imagine he wanted any more but the simple fact of being told he couldn't, that this was against god's will in some way, made him resent Anthony, for taking away all his unborn children.

The driveway was narrow and reached around the side of the house, so my father would enter and park to the left of the front door but to leave he'd have to reverse around the side of the house and then make his way down the driveway. This time Anthony was running down and reaching the side of the house where my father had disappeared only a few moments before. At the same moment my father reversed round, too fast, and there were two distinct sounds. The first was the back of the car hitting against Anthony—it was a heavy sound, like that bell in the church that an altar boy has to strike while the priest talks, but muffled, like a cloth lay on top of the bell. The second was Anthony's head whacking against the pavement. It sounded exactly like the first hit of a cleaver on a coconut. I have never rid myself of that sound but each time I tried to explain it I couldn't, not until I moved to Australia and I spent three months travelling, and on a beach in the Philippines I first heard it. The simple, steady thwack of the cleaver on the coconut. Anthony's head cracking on the pavement.

I was the first at his side, the first to see a steady syrupy crimson leaking from behind his head. That was death and at eight I understood it completely. One second someone can be running around a corner and the next they are not and never will again. And just like that the Jenga piece that kept the whole tower upright was taken, and pieces fell here and there, scattered with nobody to pick them back up. I noticed my mother disappearing in the weeks that followed. I searched for her everywhere. She was like a sun constantly setting behind buildings.

'How are you holding up?' I asked Timmy in the garden, reaching my hand out, palm facing to the sky.

'Fine, well enough. I keep thinking of Anthony, though.' He put his hand in mine.

'I don't think I ever stopped.'

'I know what you mean, but now it's like he's gone all over again, or something. Like he died with them.'

His silence again then. I drank the rest of my wine, as did he.

'Should we head back in?' he asked.

'Suppose we should, but Tim, have you thought about what they're all talking about inside?'

'Not really, to tell you the truth.'

'You should, I know it means something to you. Don't let Paul take everything and don't let Francis just decide for you.'

'Paul's not that bad, Kate, neither is Francis. What does it really matter anyway, they're just things.'

He got up first and I followed him back inside, looking at how his shoulders slouched, at his shadow that followed, getting smaller with each step.

Back inside Maggie filled my glass and went to the fridge.

'There's no more wine.'

'I wouldn't mind a whisky,' Timmy said.

'Me too, lots of ice.' I said.

Francis coughed. Maggie went into the sitting room, came back with a bottle of Jameson and left it on the table. Then she left again and came back with six tumblers, three in each hand. Her days of working in the bars. We had both worked in the same bars around the village. Known for being chatterboxes but also for being hard workers. Maggie took a large ornate bowl from the island in the kitchen—it had probably held peaches and pears—and filled it with ice and sat back down with us. She served us all large ones.

'Remember the time,' Paul started and went into a story about dad nearly choking on the Communion bread. We had never really got on, Paul and myself. When I was born, I must have stolen something from him but I never knew what. He knew how to tell a story, though, even banal stories were made funny when he told them. Soon we were all laughing. Each of us started different stories, sometimes finishing them, other times being interrupted and forgetting what it was we were talking about. All of them skirted around Anthony, they were all well before he died, or well after.

We touched upon the church too, the older ones laughing now at dad's large donations—enough time had gone by for them not to be angry anymore. For me, and I think for Timmy, too, it was still sore. Our holiday money was better spent helping the church help the less fortunate. New clothes didn't matter, sure the house was full of clothes, we should even get rid of some, he'd said, asking us to clean out our wardrobes for anything we didn't use. I had found plastic cups and string. I used to try and make things out of nothing. Papiermâché and macramé. Nothing ever really lasted though. I had taken a scissors and pierced a little hole in both cups, knotted string between them and ran across the hall to hand Timmy a cup.

Back in my room I felt the string tighten and I spoke into my cup. *I'm not giving anything away.* Then I waited. A vibration at my ear with his words coming back, *me neither.* I lay on the floor and we continued talking, each telling the other of all the things we would not do until I felt the string go flaccid and my dad's voice called us both out into the corridor where I saw the string cut in two and my dad's hand holding a scissors. I held one cup with loose string; Timmy held the other.

It wasn't just that, though, it was time, too. Mornings and evenings, Saturdays and Sundays. On the board for something, a speaker for something else. The church took him from us and left us with our mother, who was our mother no longer. All of the love drained from her. Soon after Anthony was taken, she started her weekly walks to the charity shops. Once she came back with Matryoshka Dolls. Opening each one to find another smaller one inside, until she got to the smallest one that never opened. Then she'd close each one in on the other and start opening them again.

When the subject got back to the formalities of filtering through the leftovers of our parents, I looked out the window and tried to see what my father had seen in the green, declining hills. I didn't listen much as Francis took notes and made calculations. I thought instead of how different we'd all be if six were still seven. We sat around the table, each of us cut off from one another, unable to really say what we wanted; unable to be heard. I imagined picking up a plastic cup and shouting into it with only my echo to answer me, muffled.

THE BELL, THE LIGHTHOUSE AND THE CARDS
Michael Farry

I rang the mass bell at Dromard one Sunday.
A granduncle I think, on the Kilgallon side
invited me to summon the congregation.
I went back there last year. Automatic now
so I couldn't re-enact my moment of control.
I should have climbed the hill, checked if
the far-off lighthouse still guarded the bay.
I would have had to wait for darkness.
The cottage gone, and the front gravel
the sheds, the wall and the path up the hill.
And that small china cup they gave me.
Every summer I seem to remember.
The same one, a painted robin on the side.
I may be mistaken. I'm certain of the view
from the front door. After dark you knew
where to look. The lighthouse a landmark.
Each July we relearned its signal.
Father cycled down each August, took me home.
Happy to go and happy to return.
I can still smell the sea from ten miles.
At home the mountains were in the way.
I never asked, she never said. I thought
they were all so happy, sunshine daily
and the travelling shop on Thursdays.
Fuchsia ringed the dunghill, he showed me
how to find the nectar at the neck.
What makes me wonder now is why.
Are my memories deficient? I try hard
to recall rain, loud words, flung insults,
slammed doors, fail. There was a Sunday,
rain danced all afternoon on the gravel
so we played cards on the kitchen table
and I learned the intricacies of Twenty-Five,
the right order: five, jack, ace of hearts,
high in red, low in black, trumps and tricks.
I can still hide my glee when a dealt hand
promises a sweep. I think I have a photo
of that granduncle who rang the bell
for years. I should have taken after him.

VEHICLES
David S. Higdon

We hung heads out the back window
of a Buick, wind rushing, blushed cheeks,
crouched in the floorboard the nighttime
dad drove, calloused knuckles on the wheel,
or those early mornings, to polling stations,
donut shops, bank drive-thrus, tellers gift
lollipops through pneumatic tubes.
Or weekends we packed gear for fishing
in Grandad's rusted, but reliable truck
pressed close to Mamaw, her sparrow
bones poking us through vellum skin—
we visited the grave of a great uncle, a man
we never knew. Almost adults, we piled
in the beds of pickups, we parked late
on trestle bridges, covered in country dark,
silent except for bubbling creek, we awoke
little hungry bats. There were no places
to go, not really, steamed windows and slick
seats—naked bodies fly to bright places.
Afterward, the radio filled quiet gaps.
What is it about vehicles—the feeling,
that last real freedom while the rest of life
loses air? American identities like a print
smudged on the pavement of a back road.

THAT AUGUST
Julia Deakin

The sixties – word reached us up the M1
from Fleet Street, Broadcasting House
and Telstar – were disposable. On *Blue Peter*
Valerie Singleton modelled a paper dress.

The space age was jet-propelled, everything good
was modern and everything modern
was orange, plastic and throwaway: razors,
flowers, cups, clothes. At fairs people paid

to smash shelves of china with bean bags, pianos
with sledgehammers and the crowds cheered;
in towns wrecking balls swung at streets
which bulldozers swept into smouldering piles.

After that half-hour chat with Sheila's dad
idling his Wolseley on the quiet A52,
Dad said again that we had to be *ruthless.*
Throw out everything not used in the last year:

the Manchester house would be smaller.
Later he lit a fire and down the grass path
hauled boxes, a tea chest, furniture.
Mum seemed not to mind – to be in on it, even.

Hoarders, though? Make-do-and-menders?
Crackling, odd pops. Smoke pricked my eyes.
It wasn't November the fifth. By then
it would be dark and we would be gone.

Flames licked round a black silk Victorian gown –
some old aunt's I hadn't known, tipped
from a cupboard sixty-six years past her century.
Wind crinolined the skirt which rose and fell

like lungs, before Dad threw on more stuff
even the blaze seemed to baulk at.
A trunkload, then the trunk itself.
Sparks hung in the Staffordshire dusk.

GHOST
David Murphy

A man offers you a lift, a welcome gift of a wet night.
His black-shirted forearm slithers over;
a hand fidgets in the glove compartment for a CD.
That voice still twangs in your ears
from his earlier country ballad at the wedding.

Embrace the voice in the speakers – diversion
from enforced car-bound companionship –
and wonder out loud who lurks beneath the skin
of the disc – a dead Stetson-wearer?
'No, that's me,' he blurts; a tiny smile burns his lips.

Two voices – one real, one recorded –
ignite a flare in your head. You hunt
for your tongue without finding it, and must fight
the urge to make a sideways lunge for freedom
through the metal barricade of his car.

You sit and endure, trying to believe
both his voices are as warm and melodious
as the worn-out insides of old violins. Five miles later
you wave from the flagstones and watch the departure
of a man alone with the ghost of his own voice.

In darkness something grasps the edges of your eye.
Catch your breath: a shooting star rips across the sky.
Above you, his long dead wife listens to his recording
of her favourite song, but you only have ears
for the silent music of the galaxies.

Extract from White / Other
Fran Lock

… the work of their whiteness
is covert, unconscious even, semi-conscious; invisible, refined
and sly. but they do say "chav," don't they? not to my face,
not usually, but they say it. and they do say "pikey." not
british or irish, but both and neither. to look at i am so
white that i disappear daily within the dense crush of their
anglophile assumptions. yet i live within those categories as
an alien other: strange, estranged inside of whiteness, because
they don't mean me when they say "white." for them,
"pikey" is a way of removing me from that select community
of whiteness, a form of lexical cleansing. "pikey" is also an
eviction, a banishment, a get thee hence, a spell of protection.

PHOTO ESSAY
Rebecca Moseman

A COLLECTION OF PORTRAIT PHOTOGRAPHS BY REBECCA MOSEMAN: *THE IRISH TRAVELERS, A FORGOTTEN PEOPLE.*

"Irish Travellers are an indigenous minority who, historical sources confirm, have been part of Irish Society for centuries. Travellers long shared history, cultural values, language, customs and traditions make them a self-defined group, and one which is recognisable and distinct. Their culture and way of life, of which nomadism is an important factor, distinguishes them from the sedentary (settled) population."

— Text from the Irish Traveller Movement website (itmtrav.ie).

A young traveller stands in the hallway of her family's home, ready for school.

Two brothers and their baby sister wait for their mother to finish setting up her station to sell various goods at the Ballinasloe Horse Fair.

A young traveller sits within her family's deserted caravan. One of 8 children, the family lives within a roadside encampment in Cashel.

Barbara, a young traveller mother, living within the Long Pavement halting site, sits in her caravan and comforts her baby.

A pony stands in his stall within the Ballysimon halting site. Many travellers attend various horse fairs around Ireland to buy and sell ponies.

A young girl attending the annual Ballinasloe horse fair with her family for the week takes her dog outside of her family caravan for a walk.

JJ, a young teenage boy who lives in the Craughwell halting site sits at the kitchen table within his family's caravan, surrounded by family members as he asks questions about American life and trends. While some families living in Craughwell halting site community are Deaf, JJ and his siblings are not.

Two brothers coral their ponies from the field surrounding the halting site.

Three sisters stroll around the streets of Ballinasloe during the annual horse fair with their babies.

Chantal sits with her family's caravan while her siblings play outside. Chantal's family live alongside the road rather than within a halting site.

A boy who lives within the Craughwell halting site for the Deaf poses with his hurley.

Katlyn, age 5 arrives home to her family after school.

WAFER

Trelawney

Along cold-lit aisles of the vaulted present,
every week look on as others, swift
in their certainty, get what they need.

I may be carrier to a split bag with a shrinking
collection. Past the old factory reflections,
echoes of less hapless times. Think I was kneeling

height to a man, shoulder to my nan. A post-
peasant fifties pre-fab, ragged and worn shag
rugs over cracked linoleum. Words I guess

now that some call poverty, then were so rich.
Were those stale vinegared crisps, twist-tied,
were they shuffled aside to make way for pink

wafers drawn shakily, from the bag here,
and offered to my youth. For I'm sure
those with trolleys full don't need to linger

as they stroll from the altar, or wonder
what when the wafer doesn't work.
Called upon one too many times,

the body of a vision chewed paper thin,
blood trickling into diminished scenes
seldom dreamed these days. But here,

here is a list of what you haven't lost.
An old receipt, bringing life to last week.
It was, and is, a communion in its way.

Caesar's Ceiling
Louise G. Cole

Grief splits me open, spits uneven pieces
into church, sinks me to unworn knees
to rediscover faith, pay homage to bleeding
hearts, blue-robed Mary robbed, her poor
bloodied boy spread-eagled in an agonising
death-scene detailed for my redemption.

I while away my mourning, pass Mass
making pictures from the cumuli above
the altar, ceiling-painted: there's a kitten,
Minnie Mouse, a helicopter, kites in flight,
a snarling wolf, and there, as if embossed
on a shining silver denarius, the familiar

Roman-nosed profile of my stern father
Emperor Corti, revered, exalted, missed.
Weekly I return, wear the pew to a shine,
try to pray in half-remembered words.
I talk the talk, sing in the choir, bake cakes
for coffee morning communion with

neighbours who are otherwise strangers,
until a new parish priest blows in,
from the high pulpit demands his flock
dig deeper, visits to the sick and elderly
cost dear in diesel, duty decries we give, give.
Staring above this corpulent cleric's head,

I can no longer see my ceiling Caesar's
silhouette, so I absent myself to wander,
wonder if the priest drinks or gambles,
smokes or womanizes his stipend when later,
he decrees volunteer cash counters no longer
touch his stash of paper money envelopes,

four-times-a-year gifts for deserving clergy.
One last look above the altar and I see nothing,
only emulsion. I shrug off guilt on holy days
and Sundays, even Christmas and Easter,
unremarked by everyone, anyone, no-one
until months later, in the Post Office queue.

The priest enters, but I can't make eye contact,
instead, intone politely 'Good Morning Father'
with disingenuous respect honed as a convent
teen passing Reverend Mother in the corridor,
programmed for automatic genuflection.
I try not to flinch when the pompous papist

nods without recall, sees me as a stranger
unworthy of remark, expects to queue jump.
I see he's still rotund, red-faced, dead-eyed,
driving a luxury model car, nothing cheap,
chaste or obedient, a parody of the dead man
hanging below his painted church clouds.

Holy Water
John Paul Davies

When I was ten Grandad made me a coffin –
bone-white, six inches long. Cushioned lining
nestled a Dracula in dinner jacket and cape.

Smattering of red about his blanched face
betraying a recent feed, the vampire manikin
rose on thin wires when the lid was unlatched.

All I can remember when I'm shown yours,
ushered by the nurse into a strangely narrow room
where you've been placed on an old school-chair.

A nun lurks with literature confirming your soul.
In the half-raised sash window an alabaster Christ
overlooks the Children's communal plot.

Presented with a phial of holy water,
I sprinkle the lot – ignorant of procedure –
across the toy casket in a broken vertical line,

watching blessed water drip onto overly-bleached tiles.
Only thinking later I should've wetted a finger
to make the cruciform watermark, only thinking later

of liquid cells seeking each other in darkness,
droplets quivering before pooling,
of burgeoning life out-sprinting the elements,

the primordial hungering for a simple hug.
Of you, waiting in contained gloom
to rise on thin wires at the lid's opening.

OUT-OF-SEASON
Donal McLaughlin

I.

Mid-November, Scotland, & at next to no notice: a 6-day walk.

With Ally. A friend of a friend. A *character*, if nothing else.

Glasgow to Fort William. Ninety-odd miles of the West Highland Way. *Milngavie* to the Fort, to be exact.

One foot in front of the other, anyhow. Six *days* of it.

I'm on, as a sub, for someone else.

Thirty years on, what you remember –

Milngavie to Balmaha: arriving at a forest as night fell; deciding to backtrack to the road.

Balmaha to Inversnaid: dancing, from rock to rock, along the loch.

Inversnaid to Crianlarich: waterproofed from head to toe; up to the knee in bog.

Crianlarich to Inverornan: trees, here & there only; slanting.

Inverornan to Kinlochleven: the Devil's Staircase after lunch; then the endless descent; the village in & out of view, over & over; the repeated threat, as light faded, of rushing water to cross.

Kinlochleven to the Fort: the steep-steep climb, first thing.

That final day, also: Ally's antics, at the top.

The energy he squandered, kicking bloody stones.

Snow beginning to fall. A blizzard threatening.

The feeling you should've got out while you could.

II.

What I remember most is Kinlochleven.

Mrs Aldred. Elsie Aldred. *Elsie.*

The B&B. – A council house, we're talking. Former, probably. *Bought.* A hall that, when the door opened, was the width of the front door by the width of the front door.

We're walking the Way, we say. Spotted your card in the shop. Would've phoned, we wee-white-lie (we *turned up* deliberately), but the shopkeeper insisted you were *literally* round the corner.

Oh, that's only in summer, the woman starts to say. We ought to have thought to remove the card, now that it's out-of-season.

Ally's eyes work their magic. The door – slowly – opens.

As long as you appreciate, it won't be much of a breakfast. I've nothing in. Not the ingredients for the kind of breakfast I'd normally cook for you anyhow.

Not a problem, we insist. We need a bed for the night just. A roof…

Away on up then. The first door on the left is the twin.

Help yourselves to a shower, she calls after us. You'll see the bathroom, the door's open. And come down afterwards, for a cuppa.

We wouldn't want to impose, we try to say. It's bad enough disturbing your Sunday night…

You're *not* disturbing it. No: come down, I'll enjoy the company. If you can be bothered, that is, with an old fogey like me –

We agree to come down. Will enjoy the company too.

I'm sick of this one anyway, I joke – before Ally can.

We reach the door. Pile in. I claim the bed on the left. Ally, the one on the right. It's either his turn for the first shower, or he's just the first to claim it. His boots & jeans are already off anyhow when there's a knock. It's not that he's not decent, Ally nods for me to go though.

It's Mrs Aldred, wondering would we like her to bring us a cuppa *up* first? To warm us up while we're changing. The invitation to join her would still stand.

With all this tea on offer, I'm forced to come clean.

I'm not a tea-drinker, to be honest, Mrs Aldred. But Ally is. I'll just check if he wants one.

They can hear each other, of course, but I go through the motions of being the messenger. Ally confirms he'd like a cup & I tell Mrs Aldred, he'd love one.

She can see the funny side. I can tell.

Don't worry about me, I add. I never have coffee at this time of night anyway.

She heads back down & we return to getting ready.

Before long, there's a second knock & again, *I* go over. Open the door to a Mrs Aldred, this time with a tray. There's a big mug of tea on it. A jug, sugar bowl, biscuits.

The biscuits are for me *too*, she stresses. I'd offer you a glass of milk but then there'd *really* be nothing for breakfast.

That's kind, I say, nabbing the only bourbon. Ally-boy, methinks, can have the custard creams. Don't worry about the milk. Really: don't be worrying about anything. I'll just give this to Ally…

Side-stepping boots & rucksacks, I walk carefully towards him. Ally reaches out to take the tray.

Got it?

Yeah —

Before I get back to the door though, his tea goes for a slide.

SHIT!

The whole tray flips. Mug, jug, bowl, bikkies, all crash to the floor.

He's gone 'n' dropped it, I report, needlessly.

Sorry, Mrs Aldred, Ally calls out to her. I dropped it! After you being so good, and making it for me. — Apologies for the *lang-widge,* by the way!

Something else flips & he dissolves into laughter. She's soon helpless too, on the landing.

That's *hilarious,* she chokes. — *He's* hilarious!

It's the best night she's had, she says, in Kinlochleven *ever.*

Fifteen minutes (not even) & Ally & her have *clicked.* Through a half-open door, somehow, the two of them have clicked.

Anyway: mess cleaned up — It's okay, *we'll* do it! — it's a case of: Ally, first shower; me, the second; & by the time I get down, Mr Reid has his Size 10's firmly under the table.

It's Ally & Elsie now.

I introduce myself as Martin. Not the (then) usual Marti. *Martin.*

I'm right: it's not a Scottish accent I'm hearing. It's Yorkshire. She & her husband moved up when they retired. Had always loved Kinlochleven when they came on holiday. So yeah: once they retired... Their daughters & grandchildren still come up. The B&B thing is just for extra money.

It's not a proper business, Elsie says, with a vague wave round. I don't even have a breakfast in, for emergencies. Will *never* get Tourist Board approval at this rate.

She has *our* approval, for sure. Can have every star going. Forget the poor heating & piffling shower. We'd no joy at all with the numbers in the leaflet, but *she* opened the door, let us in.

Aye: the craic that night was great. Ally & her really hit it off. He'd only to bloody look at her, to set the woman off. To have her laughing & laughing & laughing. He'd have gone on all night if she'd not said at some point:

You two will want to get to bed. You've had a long day. And have the climb out of here ahead of you tomorrow. That & the final stretch, down to the Fort. Vlad, unfortunately, is still not back. I hope he doesn't disturb you, coming in. It's a wonder you didn't notice him round in the pub, actually.

We were hardly in, we said. The coin box is just inside the door. There were people drinking, yeah, we didn't stay though.

Is he Russian? was the question not being asked. We settled for assuring her there was *no way* he'd disturb us. Totally out for the count, we'd be. Giving it major Z's.

The expression was new to her.

Major Z's! she laughed.

She pointed through to the kitchen, where breakfast would be served.

No, really, don't be losing sleep over it, we insisted, or tried to, as the apologies threatened to start all over again.

I wonder if the shop would have some things? If I nipped round in the morning…

She shopped in 'the Fort' normally. Fort William, or Inverness.

That's where I'll be anyway: the grocery store. No further than that. If you come down and see no sign of me, I mean.

We hugged her goodnight. It had been that kind of evening.

Then it was up those bloody stairs again. Limbs, blisters, cuts, all protesting.

We weren't to know, but we were the ones who'd lose sleep.

No, that's not fair: Elsie was disturbed too. Difference being: *she* half-expected it, probably.

Problem arose when Vlad came home & clomped his way upstairs. *Fee-fi-fo-fum,* it wasn't. It was clomp-bloody-clomp-bloody-clomp though.

Ally, I took it, was giving it major Z's. Being the first to nod off, all week.

Our hosts through the wall, I could hear now, were at the foot of our bloody beds, practically. You wouldn't have known with Elsie, previously. Clomp-clomp Vlad wasn't one for sneaking in though. For undressing quietly & slipping into bed. No, Vlad was a man with a grievance. Some huge, bloody grievance he'd dragged home.

That *cunt* so-'n'-so. Who the fuckin-fuck does he think he is?

The thin wall was blurring his words. Or he was slurring them, unaided.

When he finally stopped for breath, Elsie announced they'd guests.

Two young lads, walking the Way. Very nice too. They're next door in the twin, so keep the noise down.

When Vlad didn't; *wouldn't;* Elsie made the mistake of saying shush.

Who the fuck are *you* tellin to shush? Tell me again. Go on, fuckin dare ye! Tell me a-fuckin-gain to fuckin shush 'n' see where it fuckin gets ye!

There was a silence, then:

Why the fuck did ye let them fuckin in? May to September, we do. That's the agreement: May to fuckin September. An' the end o fuckin September was six weeks ago!

Likes of that continues, for minutes on end.

Any more, I decide, & I'll have to wake Ally. We'll have to burst in & get between them.

Some craic Ally-boy is, I'm thinking, *sleeping* through all this — when:

Marti? Are you awake? he whispers over.

Yeah.

Are we going in?

Not yet. But if he lifts a finger to her, we are.

Some sight we'd have been. Me bollock. My Y's, slipped off in bed, round my ankle – *if that*. Ally in the Indian nightshirt-thing his sister bought him in Delhi.

Vlad must've conked out, thankfully. Wreaked the usual havoc, then passed out.

Radio silence it was, suddenly, anyway.

If Elsie was lying there sobbing, we didn't hear her.

Us two rolled over. The room relaxed too.

Soon I was hearing major Z's.

The next morning, I'm glad to hear, Vlad leaves for work early.

Going down, he's quieter. Would pass as normal, nearly.

I snooze a bit. Ally, I reckon, is sleeping still.

I get up when I'm ready. On the way across to the window, see Ally's beaten me to it.

I open the window. Breathe the mountain air in. The *stillness*.

I arrive, down in the kitchen, to the Ally & Elsie Show. Boy *definitely* has his feet beneath the table.

Elsie, I see, is thrilled. Has found a back-of-the-cupboard sachet she didn't know she had. Hot, steaming coffee's plonked in front of me.

I reach for the milk. Discover there's none. Ally's used it all on his Krispies.

I wind him up for the hell of it.

Elsie's face drops. Best o craic or not, she's not for laughing.

I'll nip round to the shop, lads, for some! They'll have *milk* at least.

There's no stopping her. Our no-need-for-that's fall on deaf ears. As does any insistence, I can drink the coffee black.

No: suddenly the apron's off & her coat, hat & scarf are pulled on.

She looks nervy. Very nervy.

Vlad *has to* have milk in his tea, she's insisting. He can't drink it without it.

Vlad, in other words, was upstairs still.

It was comical, cept it wasn't. Two big lumps of lads giving it:

You're right, Elsie! *Go! Quick!* Aye, go 'n' get some quick –

Fast-forward an hour, tops, & that, it turned out, was the only allusion that morning to what happened during the night.

That & the great big hugs Elsie got as we left.

The one mine *became* anyhow.

MEMORY

Claire Hennessy

for a friend who digs wells

My mobile phone has a 1.2GHZ Dual Core Application Processor
and sixteen gigabytes of user memory
and all I know really is that I carry
the world in my pocket.

In my wallet there's still one
Metro pass from a pack of ten,
tucked in behind my Leap card,
a paper sliver fluttering onto the Luas platform.
I can't help saving it each time.

It's been weeks since Paris,
days out of ordinary life,
pulling all the threads from the screen back-and-forth
into the air between us, over pink wine on half-canopied tables.
We solve the problems of men and work and the world
in theory, in person,
before you go back to really saving the world
and I go back to whatever the hell it is I do,
and when the little white ticket kisses the ground again
I retrieve it
and all I know really is that you can carry
a lot in something weightless.

THE CHEMISTS
Donna Morton

You can find me here, like a faithful pet.
Love pounded in & sprouting bush.
Saliva slipping, la bouche jeweled & wet.
Darling, rough hands knead plump flesh.
Seize tenderly, destroy your petite coquette
With vigor, in routes of disastrous touch…
Howling cries we cherish, & dare not shush
Unfurling such music, our love's vignettes!

Dans le matin, we birth ourselves on fire:
Inflamed, plasmic streams patiently boil.
We combust biological, we baste
Lusty organs baked in grief's desire.
Our flavors dissipate, our love unspoiled
Find us hovering, molecular saints…

PERRAULT'S WOLF
Tracy Gaughan

Perrault warned well-bred ladies not to speak
with ill-bred men, especially if they met them
in the woods. He warned them away from
lonely forests with their ancient, perishing
trees – the wolves that may be lurking there
in tangled weedgrown tracks and ferny
underbrush. Stick close to well-known paths,
keep good form, mind your manners
and never peep into other people's
corners. He never mentioned the weather.

But I remember a distinct dolphin
skinned sky, sun a feeble flashlight behind
a voile curtain and a sheen of cobble
in sewing pin showers, skimming past in
thin sheets like transparent bible paper.
I took some cake and butter home
and standing at the door, tap, tap, soaked
through in my little red dress, I could have
raised the passions of Christ.

Pull the bobbin, he said, and the latch will go up.

He disliked me in red. (How is a woman
in red a sin, but a man in a papal
mozetta a martyr for love?)

Put the cake on the stool and get into bed with me.

I'd never feared intimate spaces,
where we die only of politeness.
So, I rose from my dress, aphrodite
from the wave and he was on me. What big
arms, I thought, what big eyes, I remembered
because I was defenceless inside them,
a solitary star inside a vast

ruined cosmos. Outside, a woodcutter
bow sawed a larch but the big ears heard no
heart snap, no wishbone break. Only bible paper
rain on the glass, tap, tap. The sun, too weak
under turbulent clouds. Big legs wound tight
around me like a bandage on a corpse.
What big teeth! A tumble down the trapdoor
of his throat and into a moral:
Perrault's wolf is already in the house.

ALL YE FAITHFUL
Jess Smith

My good friend Kit is concerned. She says
my neural pathways are still greased, that
intrusions can just skate right in. *As if,* I say
to her, *my anxiety cervix was lubed up
by a bad man.* Now I have to raise
a good one. What they don't tell you
about a cesarean is that you are strapped
naked to a leather table. What they do tell you
is that you are awake. You are awake
when they take out your intestines. You are
awake when they stuff them back in. You are
awake and strapped and naked. *Christmas
is next week,* the father of your son whispers
in your captive ear, *just think of all the twinkling.*

from "Birth: A Heroic Crown"

SALT
Leah Saint Marie

Even before we're born there's the taste of salt: the way our fathers sweat as they made us, the hard rim of the cervix, the horned shell of our body collapsing.

Then later, the sharp taste of ocean as we kiss; a palace of spice—the trade route to ecstasy.

Then later still, it's the private flavor of our grief when our kingness caves. We know what the widow knows, we share the same pillow.

It rings our body citadel—here in this oneness, millions—even in fire the fine grains drop from us as rubies.

WAITING FOR THE BABY
Afric McGlinchey

for my daughter, Micaela

You're standing on sharp shingle
littered with ashy, upside-down feathers
                              and plucks of blond marram,
which is why one boot has picked up something foreign,
          which is why you crunch when you run

Your hands are conducting an arc with a stick
                    like the parabola of a flight through time,
to the day after tomorrow's Teddy and Raf
who'll gaze obligingly upwards as you play *maybe I'll throw*
– a song they know well – and the younger one yelps the refrain

While apprehension flutters around your nightly non-sleeps,
like a bluebottle trying to find somewhere to settle,
every day, as you look up at the cliff bellying out over the ocean,
optimism bursts out of you
                              like a horse from its stall

BEFORE THE ONSLAUGHT
Martin Mc Carthy

It is a squally morning in September,
and on the pavement outside my window,
a blonde woman and a blonde girl –
presumably her daughter – are walking
steadily towards the schoolhouse.

Both are dressed in pink,
and the girl has a matching satchel
with an image of *My Little Pony,*
which explains to some degree
her own neat ponytail.

At the corner, near the traffic lights,
there is a shop with a sheltering canopy,
and they stop there, so that mother
can button the girl's small jacket
against a slowly coming onslaught.

Yet, neither seem in a hurry to hurry
that moment, and move on into the rain,
or into the whole rest of their lives –
where, already, a small scattering of cherry leaves
is being trampled in a nearby puddle.

CHRISTINE
Deirdre Crowley

When she closed her eyes, Christine went back to the dream of her singing in Detroit. On stage under the sharp heat of the lights, she watched herself glow. Wearing a white taffeta embossed dress to the knee nipped tight at the waist, her bare toned arms silky coffee-coloured. Clutching the diamond-encrusted microphone, she poured her soul into the lines, "Life ain't life until you live it," belting out each note with shut eyes as if communing with a higher power, conveying effortlessly that elusive sense of perfection that sometimes happens when melody connects with soul. The audience was mesmerised, caught up in the hypnotic power of perfect sound, some swaying along with the tune, others glassy-eyed with love. When she finished singing, she bowed her head, and whispered to the audience that she was dedicating her last song to her beloved friend Florence. Looking into the crowd as if searching for someone, she spoke the words slowly "Someday, someday we'll be together." Hot tears fell on her cheek, and she was glad she was not wearing mascara. Tears had no effect on fake eyelashes, even though they could drown a heart. In real life she had never mastered the art of mascara. It always smudged around her blue eyes, making her look ill. But in this dream, in this clip of her other life on stage, nothing stained, nothing bled or broke. This Christine was flawless.

A young dietician disturbed her. She had a runny nose and bony hands that fiddled with a clipboard and pen. She sat close, next to the bed, interrogating Christine about what she ate. Christine said she ate everything, said she cooked three meals a day, and went into elaborate detail about her menus. "Oh, no," she'd answered emphatically, when the young woman had asked if she ever found herself skipping meals, or simply forgetting to eat. Christine was secretly thinking that the dietician looked a bit flat herself, maybe she was the one forgetting to eat.

In recent weeks Christine had been struggling for sleep. For the first time in her life, she was afraid of the dark. Since the night she spotted the three men on Kelly's roof, she needed lights on all the time. They seemed to be making a movie, but this was the time of year when the Kelly's went on holidays and she became convinced that they were planning to break in. They had one of those big spotlights, which switched on and off like a winking lighthouse, and even in the dark, she did not like the look of the men, the youngest of them, especially, the one who appeared under the spotlight the most. Karl, the neighbour who lived in the house right next door, had recently left to live with his daughter in Dublin, and the young couple who had moved in never seemed to be there. Christine had phoned the Guards about the men on the roof. It was awful to be taking advantage of people when they were not there, she said. But there seemed to be no follow up at all. Then, a few weeks before she was taken to hospital, she had found all her old records again. It was like being reunited with long-lost friends. As a girl she wished she'd been born black. The only black people she had ever seen were the ones she learned about in school from the African Missions magazines the nuns sold. They were always talking about the black babies of Africa. Sister Ita, her mother's only sister, had gone to Uganda to help save the children from starvation and never came home again, not even at Christmas. Christine didn't blame her; the weather was better there.

As a teenager Christine spent hours trying to fix her hair into the high bobs of Florence Ballard, her favourite singer. She had the record cover of "Where did our love go?" propped up next to the mirror while she played the tune over and over on her father's record player. Singing in front of the mirror, with the slim tin of hair-spray for a microphone and a white towel draped around her body as an evening gown, she knew she looked and sounded better when she mimed. Back then she used to fantasise about forming her own vocal female group with Margie and Evelyn, her two best friends. She would call the group *Christine and the Mikados.* When she was growing up, her father had taken her to see many of the operas. Some were sad, others ridiculous and funny, but not the kind of thing she ever wanted to sing along with. The day of his funeral his friends from the church choir sang snippets of his favourite tunes, at the tea and sandwiches back in the house afterwards. They tipped the green leaf-patterned China teacups with the good silver spoons, to recreate the "Anvil Chorus." It sounded just like it. Barney his best friend sang "I'm called little buttercup," with a tea towel over his bald head. He pranced around the carpeted room, nearly capsizing the plates of left-over Christmas cake. Everyone laughed. But it was Ned, with the deepest voice of them all, singing snippets from "The Gondoliers," that had them all in stitches. Putting on his most refined English accent, he accentuated every lyric like a BBC newsreader, and even her mother, who rarely laughed, squealed at the ridiculous way he sang, his long face so deadpan. When Christine was asked to sing, she'd performed "Stop! In the name of love" and everyone had clapped except her mother. She could wither with a look.

The woman in the bed next to Christine was on oxygen, with two plastic tubes up her nose. Even though her lips looked purple, and she claimed that she found it hard to breathe, the woman still managed to talk incessantly, gasping her way through seemingly never-ending sentences. Christine had to listen to the long story of how she had met her husband when they were sixteen and working in The Market together. Those kinds of stories bored Christine. When the woman eventually finished the tale of how her husband had died in her arms, having choked on his cornflakes one morning after sixty years of their being together, she seemed annoyed that Christine was not crying, too. Curtly, she enquired, "And you, Christine. Is your husband dead or alive?" Christine replied that she'd never bothered to marry. She didn't want to talk about the two proposals she had declined, since they were insignificant. "You're better off, too," the woman had gasped, adding, when she could, "if it wasn't for the shame of it." People were funny the way they slighted with a smile. Christine smiled back an indifferent shrug, something she'd learned to do long ago, but the woman, seemingly not even noticing, went on about how tough times had been. "I raised three sons on little, you know. All of them have done well, plenty of money now, big houses and everything. Because we worked in The Market and got leftovers every day, they never went hungry." Many mothers saw themselves as martyrs, but the real martyrs were silent. During her years behind the counter in her father's butcher shop, Christine had seen and heard it all. He'd insisted on her working for him when she left school, taking the money and keeping the accounts. What she'd really wanted was to work in a bank or a boutique but her mother had insisted that no one would give a job to a girl with a funny foot. "In the Butcher shop you'll be someone," she'd said, and so, every day, Christine had put on a clean white coat over her neat skirts and blouses. She dressed as if she was going to a bank or boutique but spent her days taking money from customers and writing out receipts. Her father had a special stool made for her near the till, in case she got tired. At first she barely made eye-contact with the customers, but soon she grew confident. Her father would wink at her with pride as he hauled lumps of meat from the cold room to the wooden tables for chopping and boning. The two other young butchers whistled and sang while trimming and skimming meat, their bloody fingers bulging red and purple, the caked crimson impossible to get rid of. The smell and look of the dead flesh disgusted her. Even on a Sunday she could smell the cloying rawness in her hair.

Jimmy, her eldest brother, had detested the meat business, too. He'd eloped with an English girl he met at the New Year's Eve Ball in the City Hall. When the family found out later that the girl was pregnant, her parents were embarrassed, but Christine had secretly laughed at the thought of Jimmy's child having a Cockney accent that none of them would ever understand. Michael was the child's name, and it was he who now visited her every day in hospital. He threw his eyes up to heaven when she told him about the woman with the purple lips. His jaw hung open a bit until he laughed out loud, just like her father used to. The nurses were kind, except for the pregnant one who was impatient about everything. Christine thought she'd be impatient too if she had to wait for something to pop out of her. One day in the butchers', when she was still only in her twenties, she'd witnessed a woman's waters break on the tiled floor. The gush was drowned out by the woman screaming in mortification more than pain. She never came back again, not even to show off her baby, as most did to Christine, believing her to be interested in babies. But it was reported that the baby had a great mouth on him for meat when he finally started eating.

"A right little carnivore," the father boasted. Christine didn't mind older children, but babies had always frightened her. She didn't find them beautiful in their smallness and newness, as she was seemingly supposed to. Some were like wizened corpses, others looked and sounded like squealing piglets. And the stories about childbirth were enough to put anyone off. Some women who couldn't walk right after giving birth, and she had heard about many who ended up in Saint Anne's, after a fifth or sixth child, some never to return home. She used to think that if she was ever to have a husband, he'd need to look like Sidney Poitier, or better still, Muhammad Ali. Margie and Evelyn told her she'd be mad to marry Muhammad Ali because he could never be kept fed. Her father had cut out all the newspaper articles about the boxer coming to Dublin, and filled the shop windows with the photos of him eating the three steaks at the Gresham Hotel. Christine thought that he looked just gorgeous, not like the men who came into the shop, checking out their reflections in the glass window and fixing their hair before they tried to chat her up. The only black person she had seen up close was Father Al, who said Mass all that summer in St Francis church. The gold light of the tabernacle bounced off his skin, making him look like an African king on a stage. "God the father is love. All he wants for us is good things, he knows every breath we take." His voice, deep and steady, made her feel like she might explode. "He is our light and our hope; without love we are nothing." She had never heard any priest talk like that before. He floated across the altar full of grace, his movements accentuating his toned body. She imagined being his wife back in Africa, wearing those bright coloured dresses she saw in the African Missions magazines. If he were a king, she wouldn't have to carry water jars on her head. The flies in Africa would be a problem, and she knew what it was like to see and hear the viscous swarming, they trying to host on the slabs of meat delivered to the shop in summer. But at least she wouldn't need to worry about having children for him because, as king, his other wives would have given him some already. If she were to marry a black man, he'd have to look like Muhammad Ali and sing like Sam Cooke. Yet there was something about Father Al that made her rethink her plan.

Sometimes, while her father was in the back with the others, she imagined Muhammad Ali walking into the shop. But one day Father Al walked into the shop, and his smile made her melt. His eyes shone; it was as if he'd seen inside her. He looked younger up close, and even more beautiful. That night she dreamed of Father Al, and what it would feel like to have his velvet lips wandering over her body, to touch his naked chest as strong as Muhammad Ali's. When they met on the street the next week, she asked him about Africa and his home. "We can talk about Africa if you like," he said. "I could show you slides of the Mission Centre where I work." That Sunday, after lunch, she came to the parish house. She wore her favourite green satin dress, the one she'd bought in Roches Stores, and over it a long lemon cardigan so her mother wouldn't notice. When Father Al opened the door, he smiled in saying her name but seemed nervous as he led her through into the living room. The curtains were closed, and over the next several minutes the slide projector rotated, stopping noisily at each slide, throwing images of his home up onto the wall. It was as if Christine was being introduced to his family, the faces seeming to smile in approval of her. She and the priest sat on the couch in silence, staring at the images. When he did try to speak, she put her fingers gently on his lips. Then she kissed him, having never wanted anything so much. Afterwards, looking into his eyes, all she felt was love. "Next Sunday?" she asked, when it came time for her to leave. A week was an eternity to have to wait. That Tuesday, though, he came into the shop. When she saw him, her heart leapt wildly in her chest. "On Sunday I have to go to Youghal," he said. She thought for a moment and told him that she'd meet him at the station ahead of the ten o'clock train. It was simple. And she couldn't help herself; she felt called to be with him. Whatever it took, and whatever the cost, she needed more of him. But just then her father appeared at the door. "Ah, Father Al. Is it a couple of steaks you're after?" She loved the way her father made everything easy. "The steaks are on the house, Father Al," he said. "And wouldn't you come to us for your tea some evening? You'd be very welcome. Christine has a record collection you might like. Wouldn't that be nice, Christine?" There were only six Sundays left for them. The slide shows continued. Father Al visited the shop twice a week, and sometimes they pretended to casually bump into each other in O'Brien's Tea Shop, or at the cinema in the evenings. People stared. Margie told Christine the talk was that she was going to be a nun like her aunt in Africa. Christine just laughed. "Next summer I will come back as a single man," Father Al had said, one Sunday towards the end of August. Holding her tightly, he wept. "I love you, Christine. As much as I love God. He can make it happen." Such words had filled her with such hope. But that Christmas, when her father dropped dead unloading turkeys from the van, the grief overwhelmed her. And then, without warning, the letters from Africa stopped coming. For the longest time afterwards, it was as if someone had stopped the music and thrown Christine into a windowless room. Days stretched into months, and she began to feel that she'd imagined it all. In that way, summers came and went, many of them, eventually, but none felt as warm as the one she'd known with Father Al.

On her last night in the hospital, she woke to the sound of a voice calling her name. He was standing at the door, and started singing a song about home. He looked older and walked now with a limp, but he'd learned to sing just for her. His voice was chocolate; it made her feel alive again. And his eyes shone as he sang. Slowly, no longer afraid, she left her bed and took his hand for the magic of his touch. Together, then, they walked into the night. The sky was full of music, sprinkling stars like confetti all around them.

Like a Thousand Drums in the Night
Regi Claire

His good hand has found the shears, freckled with rust,
in the workbox behind his old journals. Metal legs snip-
snap in step, metal arms clamp as his fist directs, cutting
the hedge by moonlight, up and down from window
to door, along his study's book-lined wall.

Ghosts of leaves mock unheeded. His ears are empty shells,
his hearing aids someplace else. Paper smiles barely
avoid getting shredded. His glasses too are
elsewhere. Only the mirror sees, infiltrates good
or bad, and lets the door shutter-unshutter its mindless eye.

His bad hand is hot, hot, hot. It wavers, imitating the right like a broken
brother, brushes past Jung's autobiography, then a history
of archeology. Nailed above the window, African gods swallow
down the coming of dawn and out of their mouths long-silenced tribes
make thunder, thunder like a thousand drums in the night.

After Visiting the Healer

Lani O'Hanlon

A platypus, with a large flat beak arrived,
you know the platypus lays eggs but also feeds milk to her young?

Her heart was outside her body. I took it in my hand,
subtle beat against my palm as I nestled it back under her ribcage.

Blue, red, yellow and pink birds flew in through the window,
nestled in the folds of the duvet and against my breast,

when I moved so did they, flying up from the bed,
out and then back in through the window.

The children were there as well, propped up on pillows beside me.
I taught them how to be still so the birds could alight

on their heads and shoulders as they walked
away through the garden, rosehips growing above them.

DREAM CATCHER
Sinéad McClure

The day you moved the dream catcher
from the shed it had hung in for twenty years
I knew we were letting go of ourselves.

Wild things took over. Fields filled up easily.
Buttercups in May, meadowsweet in July,
purple headed self-heal a mat beneath the apple trees.

When I threw out the dying chrysanthemums
one clung to the nettle bed still breathing,
and the forest became itself again.

Now there is a cadence to our steps
and joined up writing in the sky
as we traipse the sun's long-shadow paths.

The dream catcher takes our harshest winters
holds it in nets to spin forever from the alder.

Earbuds
Alan McCormick

Seán met us at the airport in an old green Volvo Estate that looked like it had been reclaimed from the scrapyard.

Masks? I asked, before getting in.

It's okay, I had it a few months ago and I'll keep the windows open, Seán said.

You never told me.

Well, I'm good now. Grand journey? he asked, turning to Ian, who'd taken the seat up front with him.

Wish it had been grander, Ian replied. How's the weather been?

Ah, the weather? said Seán. Good for staying indoors.

Even though Seán had the windows down, the car smelled rank, of musty worn leather and damp rotting fur. As he drove, he addressed me from time to time with a glance in the driver's mirror: mundane questions about my work and about Carmel.

I became co-director last year. And she's fine. Graduating soon.

Going to be a businesswoman like her Mam, Therese?

Ian scoffed.

Not if she can help it, I replied. She wants to do something more poetic with her life.

And potentially be paid for it, Ian chipped in.

Oh, right, said Seán, being paid for anything is never a bad thing.

As Seán drove – and he drove at surprising speed which I'm sure he hadn't last time we visited – I became fixated by his sunburnt farmer's neck, so like our father's, the copper grey twists of hair twigging out of his frayed collar, the casual unkemptness and disregard for how he looked.

How's Mary? I asked, hoping she might still be doing his laundry at least.

Doing a good job of being Mary I imagine.

You imagine?

Carmel must be eighteen.

Nearly twenty-one I corrected; will be a graduate soon.

Right, you said that, sorry. I haven't seen her since she was four, it's hard to keep track.

She was six! She wanted to come this time but –

Ah, come on, I know: life's busy when you're young.

Will Mary be there when we arrive?

What did you say Carmel is studying?

I got the message to pull back on the Mary questioning: She's doing literature and art.

She'll be a teacher then, I expect.

Yes, most likely.

Or unemployed, said Ian, which made Seán laugh and drum his fingers on the steering wheel.

Well, there's always a job here helping out if she's desperate enough, he said.

And Ian and I fell silent, afraid to laugh in case he wasn't joking and might think we were being disparaging about the offer.

The roads had improved a lot since our last visit and it was noticeable how many new expensive cars people were driving. Seán continued to drive his wreck like a man possessed.

What do you think of Lewis Hamilton? Ian asked. It was a sly question.

The best Formula One driver ever, it's a shame you Brits don't appreciate him more.

When we reached the outskirts of Wicklow, Seán said he needed to get some provisions.

Come if you like, he said.

I've never shopped at a Lidl, I replied.

You've been missing out there, Therese, he said and took Ian with him.

I was about to shout a reminder but they both put masks on before going inside.

In the car park, I could see another way Ireland had changed since I'd left. There were actually people from abroad, who looked and sounded like they might live here, mainly Eastern Europeans but also some Africans and people from the Middle East; refugees probably.

Ian and Seán arrived carrying two boxes each — wine and beer.

Ian was more than generous, said Seán.

The least I could do.

Did you get any food? I asked.

Of course, some bread and potatoes, Seán replied.

Ireland hasn't changed much then?

I wouldn't know about all that now.

Okay, Father Dougal, but it does look more cosmopolitan.

He knew what I meant immediately: The Grand is a refugee hostel now.

No!

Yes, but I doubt they have room service.

It's good that Ireland is doing its bit.

Bits and pieces, but they could be doing more.

Driving along the high street, I ducked in my seat as we stopped at a pelican crossing.

That wasn't Mrs Gleason, was it? I asked after we'd safely moved on.

The very same.

I thought the old bitch died years ago.

Well, she did but they exhumed her so she could haunt the town forever.

Horrible woman, I couldn't go near a piano after she'd finished with me!

The town seemed to have been taken over by teenage girls, walking and chatting in small packs; puffer jackets, long hair, short skirts and spindly tan legs. After passing a few groups I realised their legs and faces were more orange than brown.

Is there a new sunbed parlour in town?

It's fake tan, said Ian.

I thought being orange was a traveller thing, I said.

Right there, milady, said Seán, but it's a teenage girl thing now too.

Why? I asked.

No reply was offered. Can we stop at the lighthouse? I asked, changing the subject. I always loved it there.

Of course, said Seán, sharply taking the next left turn, funnelling at speed down a tight country lane. When we passed a farm I got the smells I knew so well, the acrid stench of slurry and rotting carcasses, the piss and shit of the yard that made me retch.

Jesus, can you please close the windows?

You've never called me Jesus before, Seán said, but you'll have to wind up your window yourself, no electric controls in this car, I'm afraid.

At the end of the lane we all climbed out of the car. I tried to flick off the hairs I'd picked up on my jacket.

You still have dogs then, Seán? I asked.

I do: three of them.

Don't tell me that Beckett is still alive?

He is, though he does the running and fetching in his sleep these days.

At the lighthouse — now an upmarket holiday rental — the land opened out, bumbling hills of yellow gorse rolling down to the cliffs and sea. The air felt so good after travelling.

Seán lit up a cigarette and offered Ian one.

He gave up five years ago, I said.

I gave up five years ago, said Ian. But I'll have one to keep you company.

No you won't!

No I won't, said Ian, taking one.

I took off down the hillside; smoke plumes pursuing on the wind. At the cliff's edge I looked down to the vast caves below, birds congregating, swooping and circling over the sea, a few hovering in my eye-line on the wind's currents, their beady eyes fixed ahead.

I used to come here with Aoife and Lily (we smoked then too), me escaping the house when my mother was ill and holed up in bed.

Once Seán came on his bicycle and tried to join us.

Away, little gobshite, I told him, and both girls laughed.

You need to come home quick, he said.

Oh no, I said. Why now?

I looked back up the hill, and Seán and Ian downed their cans in one and waved at me.

The dogs, Beckett hobbling behind, his tail still remembering to wag, greeted us with wild hungry barks as we got out of the car. It was immediately obvious that the farm had gone to seed, a barn door perilously hanging off its hinges, small mounds of debris everywhere, filthy upturned buckets, an empty rusty water trough, the smells of defecation and decay ingrained into the ground, numbed by time.

An emaciated chicken purposefully crossed the yard, head extended out, twitching forward and back, as if it knew where it was going.

Ah, here comes dinner, said Seán.

Poor thing, it doesn't look like it's ever eaten, I said.

A new thing, you starve them for the pot. Fat's bad for your heart, and only the French plump them up these days.

Is that true? I asked.

I've no idea, he said. Come on let's get your bags inside.

I was about to put on my mask.

No need, we're all family here.

What's that? I said, pointing at a small tatty caravan in the corner of the yard.

Magda's place, he said.

Magda?

Magda!

Magda was waiting in the kitchen with a pot of tea and homemade biscuits. She was young, naturally pretty and confident, and looked to be very much at home.

Welcome Seán's sister and husband, she said.

Not Seán's husband, my husband, I corrected. A weak joke I immediately regretted. But she smiled and handed me a mug of tea.

Magda, I quickly learned (from my questions) was a young Estonian – she could only be 25 at most! – who'd come over with a group to help with 2019's harvest. When the others returned before the first lockdown she'd decided to stay.

You don't miss your family? I asked.

Ian stepped in: bit early for the third degree, you've only just met the poor girl. His breath reeked of smoke.

Magda's made up the bed for you, Seán said. It'll work best if I stay in the caravan; give you two more room.

I bit my tongue and tried my best to hide any shock from my expression.

Catching flies there, sis.

I closed my mouth. Well, if you're sure, I said, and Magda stared straight at me, smiled and mock-curtsied.

Our room had been newly cleaned. A rush job, dust dampened and rubbed into the grooves of the furniture, but tempered by a beautiful array of wild flowers on the chest of drawers. The drawers had been emptied, the bulging black bin liners stuffed under the bed probably holding their recent contents. The room smelled of the nineteen nineties, Harpic and cheap floral perfume. The sheets though were thankfully clean.

Seán has made an effort, said Ian impressed.

She might only be 21, and she's been sleeping in here.

Yes, Miss Marple, that might be true.

Less than half Seán's age!

I don't think she's 21: 25 at least, so not quite half.

It's not a maths problem, Ian, it's not right.

We don't know that Seán sleeps in here.

I kneeled down and pinched a hole in one of the bin liners – his jumper, I said, I remember it!

He may keep his clothes under the bed, that's all. She may have made the bed and left her scent –

I don't like the way you say 'and left her scent'.

And I don't like the way you're jumping to conclusions and judging everything.

How do we know that they've even been vaccinated?

We don't but Seán said he'd already had Covid, didn't he?

Magda's age group almost certainly won't have been fully vaccinated.

Not that again.

Or people from her country, she may not even be legal, so won't appear on any vaccination database.

Just relax!

I've told you before that telling me to relax when I'm not relaxed doesn't help!

Don't relax then.

I took a deep breath. I didn't like the way she curtsied; it was disrespectful.

I thought it was sweet.

Don't be clever!

I forgot: you're the clever one. My stupid arse is going downstairs for a drink. Your brother said the craft beers we bought –

You bought! No, I bought!

Relax! he said and got out of the room before I could reply.

I collapsed onto the bed. This had been my parents' room before my mother died and Dad absconded into the small room at the back of the house. Their bed left cold until Seán moved into the room when he passed twenty-one and I was working away in London, a rite of passage for the son who stayed, the hard slats (one still missing) of the headboard, and the tarnished brass knobs on each corner of the frame still wobbling away even after thirty years. Thankfully the lumpy sprung mattress had been updated. It felt like a cheap foam one but was comfortable at least. I lay on my back and looked up at the ceiling, the same watermark like a birthmark above the light. Jesus, the same brown lampshade, I'd always hated that lampshade! Even as a young girl, I'd moaned at them to get a new one.

Lying in the bed with my mother when she'd come out of hospital after her second stroke, I told her I'd paint the room and get her a new shade so the room would be brighter. She groaned and tightened her grip on my arm with her good hand and shaped a kiss as best she could with her lips.

The one wall I managed to paint before I left for university was still white, the rest of the room left shaded in vintage tobacco yellows and browns.

I closed my eyes. Dad is drunkenly obsessing around the rusted hinges of the gate into the cow field. He's cursing at the cold, his exhaled breath spurting out plumes of steam. He drops his tools, and then he trips. The cows murmur their discontent at his inability to let them out and charge.

I woke with a start to a lone cow clopping around the yard, and the sound of hyena-like laughter from the kitchen. As I went down the stairs, I heard chairs scraping, and as I reached the kitchen door the laughter stopped.

When I opened the door, Ian and Seán were standing by the range holding glasses full of whisky, looking shifty. Magda slinked (it's the right word) over and placed her arms around my shoulders, pulled me in and whispered in my ear: so sorry about your father, lovely person.

She meant well (I think) but I felt pangs of jealousy that this young person, a stranger, had a view on my father – even if it was simplistic, wrong – and that she had been around him in his last years. Work had been so busy and Covid lockdowns had robbed me of any chance and so I was left to…

Seán interrupted my train of thought: Magda, bring my lovely big sister over here; she looks like she could do with a drink.

Still hugging, Magda shuffled me towards them as if I were an invalid. Seán poured a big glass of red wine and handed it to me.

I pointed at the half empty whisky bottle behind him. One of those too, please!

He smiled warmly, his eyes red and watery, blearily sentimental like Dad used to get when he was drinking.

Sláinte, Therese, he said, raising his glass.

Cheers, I said, raising mine. Something smells good.

Chicken, said Ian.

Oh, God, not the —? I said, remembering the emaciated bird jittering across the yard.

Seán laughed and flipped open the bin and pulled out a cellophane wrapper as if he were a magician: Lidl's best free-range chicken! he announced. We'd never kill Mary — he clocked my surprise at the name — Mary 2 is part of the family now after Mary 1 flew the nest, God Bless her — I nodded as he confirmed my suspicions — this here is a guilt free, no kill, no fly zone, he continued, aping the voice of a hillbilly Marine, and, then, softening into his own voice: but it's also a sanctuary for abandoned strays — and he smiled fondly at Magda.

That's lovely, I said. Now, are you are going to wash your hands?

He dropped the wrapper in the bin and then licked each of his fingers in turn like a cat. Ian laughed. The alcohol will disinfect anything; don't worry.

Disgusting!

Magda looked sympathetically at me and led Seán in the crook of her arm, put on the hot tap at the sink, and gestured that he should wash.

Thanks, Magda, he said. I was being foolish.

She kissed him on the cheek. Yes, foolish boy, she said.

I noticed Magda wasn't drinking. Would you —?

No, no. Wine when we eat, she said.

Above the table on the fireplace I saw —

The urn, I see you've noticed 'it', Therese.

God, it's big.

Well, Dad was a big man.

I thought of the last video call I had with him in hospital: a nurse holding up his phone; him, shrunken and anything but big by then, breathless, unable to talk, eyes full of fear. It was only hours before they took him into ICU and put him on a respirator, the last time I'd see him. I waved goodbye and said he'd be okay. And now, reduced to this! I could feel emotion like a violent storm taking me over but I steeled myself like I did with my nerves when giving a talk, told myself to get a grip and took in a deep breath: Can we do it tomorrow? I said.

Whenever you like, the day after is fine too, they've waited to be back together all these years; another day or two won't make any difference.

No, I want to get on with it.

Whatever you say, and it's okay to cry; I could see you holding back. He walked over and put his arm round me.

God, what is it with this house and everyone touching me?

Ian had been about to come over but thought better of it, always the careful (a crueller person might say cowardly) pragmatist, he knew from experience when to get close and when to keep away. For that, at least, I'll remain forever grateful.

I drained my whisky and held out my empty glass for a refill.

As he poured, Seán showed me the label on the bottle, *Writer's Tears*, and winked.

I've started at the words again, he said.

Well, I'm sure the whisky helps.

He laughed and Magda laughed harder.

No, I'm pleased for you. You always earned good marks at school for your stories, didn't you?

Magda ruffled his hair like my mother used to.

The writing is great but I can't help noticing that the farm isn't doing so well.

What if you could help noticing?

I've sent money since the recession, and more after Dad got ill and you had to get in help.

We've always been grateful, Therese.

No need, but why this? I mean, where are the animals?

We have a chicken, two cows, three dogs.

Where's Dad's herd?

Seán had to sell, no choice, Magda said.

I was asking my brother.

Don't be rude, Therese, he said.

How are you making money?

I've saved some you sent.

It was meant to help keep the farm going.

It was generous but it wasn't enough.

What?

Your guilt money wasn't enough.

Ian made an unlikely intervention: Steady on, Seán, no need for that.

Sorry, Kofi Annan.

That made me want to laugh but I held it in: Shut up, Ian, I want to know what Seán means by 'guilt money'!

You swanned off to Trinity and then to your great career in London — not Sydney, not Hong Kong, not even fecking New York but fecking London, an hour's fecking flight away — and you visited Dad and me a handful of times in thirty years. And each time you came, you acted more like Princess Diana — and by the way, that's not meant as a compliment — and less like my sister who'd grown up on a farm, whose parents somehow found money for every fecking class she ever fecking wanted to do — French conversation, cake making, pony club, ballet, piano, orchestra, debating, Tai fecking Chi — and who had to be paid to help muck out the sheds and milk the cows.

But I never liked doing those things.

You think I did?

You could have left.

For Chrisssake, woman, I was fourteen when Mam died!

You sound like Dad there.

I'm surprised you remember. Twice he met his granddaughter, once when we came to London when she was born, and once when you brought her over when she was little more than a baby!

She was six!

I mean, did you have to make it so obvious how much it all disgusted you? How we disgusted you!

That's not fair, take that back. I never said you disgusted me.

But you behaved like you thought it. Christ, last time you came you booked yourself into a hotel in Dublin; couldn't find one good enough for you here –

Tinakilly was booked out –

All because you couldn't bear staying with Dad and me in this house.

I have an allergy to mould.

She does have allergies, Ian said.

Shut up Ian, I said.

An allergy to us more like. To Ireland, to any fecking thing you once were! All that shit sniping in the car: *ooh, they have fake tans, I've never shopped at a Lidl, look at all the travellers, refugees, potatoes.* Where did you get off on being so stuck up?

You tell me.

And when you came over to nose around and witness our feck-off-all-of-you-it's-our-turn Celtic tiger, you couldn't bear the fact that people suddenly had money and displayed, what was your expression: 'no taste' in spending it. I mean you don't have a problem in *tremendous terrific Teddington*, mixing with your spoilt-brat friends with their show-off identikit designer homes, live-in nannies they hate because they relate to their kids and husbands better than they do, four-wheel killer wagons they can't even drive, holiday homes stolen from the disenfranchised French and Italians –

I always thought you would have made a good Irish Che Guevara.

Thanks, because it is about class, isn't it, Therese? So when the Irish suddenly became middle class and started buying new cars – mostly on tick by the way – and building big arsed extensions on their dopey bungalows, going on cruises, buying apartments in the Canaries, it offended your newfound sensibilities, and you couldn't bear it, could you?

Have you finished?

Yes, I think you ought to finish, said Ian.

Shut up, Ian!

And stop telling your husband to shut up, he's only trying to protect you.

Yes, I'm only trying to protect you, Therese.

Shut up, Ian! We said together, and then looked at each other, smiles beginning to crack.

I'm going for a walk; leave you idiot siblings to fight it out, said Ian. Mind if I take a beer with me?

Sorry, Ian, take as many as you like, Seán said.

One will do, and he grabbed a bottle and left.

I've probably said way too much, Therese. But one last thing: keep Magda out of all this. She's welcomed you.

Seán mentioning her name made me realise that she must have left the room well before.

She got out quickly, I said

She knew what was coming, she's clever like that.

You're lucky to have her.

I am.

Can I ask what happened to Mary?

Mary was saved from the pot.

Ha!

Seán looked thinner than I'd seen him before, ravaged somehow.

You look tired, Seán. Are you well now?

I'm fine; it's all the ranting.

It was good, got a bit boring towards the end but I enjoyed it.

Really?

Kind of, yes, I think I did. Will you two really sleep in the caravan?

We'll top and tail, if you like.

I didn't mean –

Another drink?

Why not?

Let's take them outside; I need a smoke.

Why not have one in here?

Magda doesn't like it.

She's got you well trained.

Well, I need training.

We drank and Seán smoked. It was dark and a light was on in the caravan.

Shall I knock and ask Magda to join us?

No, Seán said. She's fine. I'd like to hear more from you.

There's nothing to say.

I've never asked you properly about your work.

You could ask now.

What exactly is it you do?

Oh, God, not tonight, maybe in the morning, as long as you have Power Point and an expensive espresso machine.

He laughed.

And I do appreciate all they did for me you know, the sacrifices they made so I could get away.

They were really proud of you, and Dad loved it when you called Carmel after Mam.

At that moment, Beckett unfurled his bones from where he was lying, stood shakily up and staggered over, dropping himself by Seán's feet. Seán knelt down and rubbed under his chin, and Beckett rolled over onto his back to offer his tummy – what he really liked – for a proper stroke.

You know the hospital told me that Dad died at 3.15 in the morning. Beckett howling downstairs had woken me in the middle of the night at that precise time, hours before the call from the hospital. He didn't eat for days, stayed under Dad's chair in the kitchen with his slippers in his mouth – he always brought them to him each morning for him to wear on the cold tiles.

Wow, I said, and started to cry.

A good old Lassie story always does the trick, eh?

What! It's not true?

No, no, it is. You cry; you need to cry.

You saying 'I need to cry' makes me want to stop.

God, you're complicated, Therese.

I didn't know whether I was laughing or crying, but it was ugly; I was probably doing both.

I'll get a tissue for the snot, Seán said, and went inside.

In the morning my head pounded. I took an Alka Seltzer, left Ian in bed and went to the bathroom. On the way back, I poked my head in Dad's room but didn't feel ready to go in, and then went into my old room next to his at the back of the house.

It was pink and white as if it was still 1990, and I was about to leave for university. The near empty bottle of 4711 left on the bedside table – that was the floral perfume smell in our bedroom! – Magda must have been sneaking a cheeky drop here and there. My childhood posters still on the walls – the holy quartet of Culture Club, Morten Harket, Nelson Mandela and Mary Robinson – still staring at each other from each wall, frozen in time.

Above my bed were photos of the family and some of my friends, alongside a series of me growing up. I looked closer, and realised that, mixed in with the photos of me at significant life-stages – just born, baptism, first bike ride, first day at school, confirmation – were complementary pictures I must have sent of Carmel passing the same milestones.

I don't know whether it had been Dad or Seán who'd curated all this together, but it was telling that, after a sour looking one of her on her first day at Grammar school, the pictures of Carmel just dried up.

I could hear barking outside. Looking out of my window, I saw the two younger dogs yelping and chasing each other around the overgrown garden. At the far end of the garden, Beckett sat looking up at Seán, who was attempting to mend a lock on the big metal gate that led out into the fields. Seán held up a series of Dad's tools to inspect them, as if he wasn't sure what each of them were meant to do. It looked like he was hoping for divine intervention, and after a while he resorted to a familiar bodger's tactic and started hammering inanely at the gate's lock with what looked like the biggest hammer he could find. It was hopeless and desperate, and yet somehow also noble and touching in its purposeful fruitlessness. I only hoped he was a better writer than a farmer, a thought I'd tell him later, hoping that he'd take it as the compliment it was meant to be.

I rang Carmel on FaceTime.

Hi, love, I said.

Hi, Mum, how's it going? Not too squalid I hope. Have you booked into a hotel yet?

No, it's okay. Listen, I know you're busy with preparing for graduation and saying goodbye to your friends.

Yes, you won't believe what Rosie has got planned —

I can imagine but, look, I'd like you to come over, we're going to sprinkle your Granddad's' ashes on my Mam's —

Mam's?

Yes, I say Mam when I'm here — on Mam's grave.

It's not a good time.

I know, but I think it's important that you come. You can get a test at Boots today, and I'll book the ticket for you to come over in a couple of days; Uncle Seán will pick you up at the airport.

God, okay, if you insist, but he's not going to be really boring, is he?

Probably, but you can always put in your earbuds; he won't even know what they are. But he might surprise you too. You have things in common: he's a writer now, and you can get to know each other on the way down.

Well, that could be interesting, I suppose, and he might even tell me what you were like at my age.

Oh, God, I hope he doesn't do anything like that. Anyway, we'll stay on for a few days; there are things I'd like to show you.

Sounds ominous.

Maybe, but I'm going to show you anyway.

TWO POEMS
Olaitan Humble

ELEGY

I remember. I remember how the simple thought of
father's death became cancer cells growing in my brain.

Father forbade elegies. So when father died, the house
fast became a colony of mutes. After my quinquennial

silence, I crossed the Rubicon. I knew exactly what I
was doing but what did I care? Funeral flowers collap-

sing in my mouth. First, I heigh-hoed to father's grave
in the black thobe he wore on the day he died. *Heigh-*

ho! Heigh-ho! Heigh-ho! What better way to challenge
the angel of death to a fashion contest. A duel lurking

in my head since the moment father was wrapped in
cheap garments & laid to sleep six feet deep as if to say:

Ye, son of Adam. Today, you are doomed! It appea-
red as though death had a special way to treat visitors.

So blame me [not] if I cut my body to pieces in the na-
me of pleasing father's dying wish. I learnt to dine with

the devil in those last moments. I learnt that breaking
bread with the gods required a longer spoon than the

one I had so I became like Johann Faust. So blame me
[not] if I sound suicidal or why does the idea of dying

never leave me be? So blame me [not] for the colour of
my thobe. So blame me [not] for the bug in my eyes.

Blame me [not]. Blame the spoon in my hand. Blame
the puddle of tears in my mother's eyes because nana

went too & never returned. Blame me [not]. Blame my
brother's loudmouth. Blame me [not] for this tattoo

on my left arm carrying father's insignia. Now may you
excuse me while I wipe these mysterious drops of moist-

ure from my eyes? Because father forbade elegies & when
he died, the house fast became a colony of mutes.

Fainted or Last Calling

Pen talks, mind confuses. What better way
to clear a head flooded with grisly images?

Perhaps waiting out the storm of uncertainty.
She allows the gentle autumn breeze to settle

on every fiber of her being. While the twitch
of her right eyelash suggests distress, she

kerchiefs her face in false cool. I offer a slap
of camaraderie between her shoulder blades.

This is just enough to restore her far-travelled
mental focus back to the realm of mortals

& for the nth time; in what appears like forever
—she feels a clutch of uneasiness. She is no alien

to this feeling. It is very challenging for me to
not be a schadenfreuder when this feeling

of hers wells up. Sometimes, it starts to erupt
into a paroxysm of rage, or desire, or catharsis,

or… but thanks to my glittering charm. Now
her voice is forged into a staccato of sonic bangs

—the sound of grace; the calling of home. The mere
thought that the world appears to have collapsed

on us careens through her mind. She says to watch
the shadow of vigor seep away from me shawls

her heart in multiple folds. She loves & wanderlusts.
Her love the touch of the heavens; the colour of peace.

She loves wholeheartedly. Her heart the spout
of klein bottles—the homecoming. Her name

a metaphor for bird. She keeps a cavalier mien
about the idea of dying. *What if you feel the*

pain of my absence deeper than the comfort of
my presence? She ponders. It is one of her

rhetoric to make me talk or say something
& each time we have a spirited discussion

punctuated by frequent raised voices, I am
gripped by pangs of conscience without

a show of an ounce of pretense or
disappointment. She loves & loves

& loves. She puts me through the
wringer when she feels insecure

during which she twinges her vermilion
borders to signalise an imminent

French kiss. It's one of the few signs
we practised before her embalmment.

13.58, January 28th 2022

James McDermott

I never planned to be at your death bed
so soon but here we are face masked cracked glass

of untouched water a wobbly stool I
cool beside your white hot bed sheets your face

a hog's your snout dribbling tubing your tongue
a red apple nurses turned you over

praying for a new leaf to drain fluid
on lungs but they couldn't so here I am

piglet at boar's slaughter they say *it's time*
to slide out snotty lines vacuum bloody

phlegm from your mouth turn off support and I
cling to your arm like a cliff edge then death

makes a Bacon painting of your boy's face
pink skin fading purple then ghost grey ice

WALKING AROUND IN SALT
Kay Sexton

On the days when nothing works, this works. Put your hand in the freezer — not just in it, but find that cliff of ice that forms when you leave a freezer door open and put your hand on the ice. Feel it melt under your fingers, then feel your fingers cramp with cold. Feel them throb with pain and then stop throbbing, stop feeling, stop being fingers altogether. Watch your nails turn blue. It's not a good blue although its name is pretty — cyanosis, it's called. Sounds like something Courtney Love might call her daughter.

Then tell your body to lift that hand off the ice. You can't tell your hand anything — it's not listening to you anymore. Kick the freezer door closed on your way to the sink. Put your hand under the hot water. It feels colder than your hand. Then it feels hot. Then your hand admits it's returned to life and it hurts. That hurt? That's life.

There are other ways to know you're alive, but most of them aren't as accessible as the freezer. You've got to be careful not to push it too far, but on the other hand, you can't be too vigilant about not pushing it far enough. That's the way to a different disaster.

After the ice you can make calls, go to dinner, sit in cinemas with dates and be alive… or at least be life-aware enough to fit in. Because fitting in is important. You need to make calls, especially to your parents who are suffering. Dinner is important, dates are important. Your parents need to see that you are living. That you are over this. Everybody's had their sorrows. And your sorrow is inappropriate.

Other things that work. Running. Swimming. Sex would work if you had the chance, but those dates don't lead to sex. Anything that exhausts the body brings you back into life's orbit. But it's tiring and on so many days you don't want to be there. You can't help wondering what it's like not to have to orbit.

It's not right to be self-indulgent. Nobody says this, but it's pretty clear that's what they're thinking. After all, it's been one of those years, two of those years now, where sorrow has been universal. Covid, Brexit, furlough… most people have lost something unimaginable. Not just you.

And it's not right to be so immoderate. Your loss hasn't been extravagant, immense, beyond reason – so why do you have this deadness?

Nobody says 'you were only his sister' but that's what they think. Not his mother, not his wife, not either of his two little kids. Only his sister. You weren't even close. They don't say that, but it's the truth.

Closeness has nothing to do with it. Or everything. Proximity. You didn't need to be close. You were proximate. Alan was seven years older, too much a big brother to be a playmate, not old enough to be a surrogate parent. He was just there from the day you were born, your earliest memories coloured by him, every experience shaded by his path preceding yours. Your bike was his old bike, the garden swing you loved was originally put up for him, your first teacher said "Alan Pugh's little sister?" Your trajectory was set by him.

When his wife, Izzy, asks you to stay for the weekend you can't imagine why. It's not like you were close. Izzy is the kind of woman who tires you out – her face, expressing every little emotion, is like watching somebody channel-surf endlessly. But it's also not like you weren't close. You've done Christmases, picnics, christenings, barbecues. You've done a lot. You've put Izzy off for over a year – not so difficult in the pandemic.

It's not her, but Ollie, her oldest son, who's invited you. Her son and Alan's. A party for his seventh birthday and you're invited as a surrogate something. Izzy knows all about surrogates. Since Alan died, your parents have called her every week about the car and the plumbing and the investment questions they used to ask him. You know because they mention it in their weekly call to you. Fully aware of what they're doing, able to imagine how hard it must be for Izzy, you've said nothing. Izzy's said nothing either.

It's odd how different the house is. His car gone, his smell absent, no male voice to counterbalance the shrillness of a woman and two little boys.

She's thin. You tried thin, it didn't work. You tried comfort eating too, but it wasn't comforting enough. Izzy's taken the birdlike approach to grief – her cheekbones threaten you when you air-kiss her. Imagine their sharpness hovering above the boys for goodnight kisses, hear the sound of a circular saw emerging beneath her skin, modulating its note as it cuts into plump childhood flesh. For somebody who never played computer games or watched horror, you have a large lexicon of unpleasantness to draw on.

Izzy's freezer compartment is ice-free and the kitchen is anyway too busy for it to be of use. They live further inland than you, so no hope of a quick ocean dip. You ask her what she does when it gets too much, but you ask gently, appropriately, over wine, after the boys are in bed. No hint of the numbness that is swallowing you alive, inch by inch, over the hours of this birthday weekend.

"I do nothing," she says grimly. "Don't need to. The longest time I've had to myself since—" she can't say his name or state the facts. " . . . eight hours. Then one of the boys wakes up – if they didn't already get up in the night for water, or nightmares or to pee or tell me that there's a fox in the garden, and it's breakfast, school run, work, school run, dinner, bed."

Izzy drinks like a bird too, but not in a pretty way, turning her over-bright eye up sideways at you as she sips. For a sipper, she can really put it away. Most of the time she's still. Like a mantis.

"No time to suffer, you see," she finishes.

Maybe you inherited the suffering and she inherited the boys and Mum and Dad's questions.

The mantis-bird hugs you before bed, and you are rigid in the guest bedroom you've always slept in, the curtains too flimsy to keep out the light, the bedlinen still smelling like it's brand new. Sleep is impossible, although you still feel nothing, not even frustration, just awareness of the gap between how things were and how they are.

At five am you give up, swing your feet down to the laminate flooring and sit, allowing the cold to strike upwards: ankles, calves, knees.

You've hired a car. It's just sitting there, in the driveway. You packed a swimsuit, although you hadn't consciously thought about why. It's an hour's drive to the coast. Nobody in this house will stir for at least that long, so why not?

Why not drive to Dover, walk steadfastly into the cold ocean, sink your uncomplaining body into the grey salt shallows? People think you're courageous or tough, but all you are is unfeeling and if you're unfeeling, why not make the most of it?

It's colder and greyer than you thought. Colder and greyer than your own bit of ocean, further west. So cold that when you wade back to shore, numb with the numbness that passes for feeling now, you can't drive. Fifteen minutes, massaging frozen feet with icy fingers, before you're safe to get on the road, although there's no way to warm your gelid skull, like something trapped in a glacier, suspended in ice. That will just have to wait until your hair dries in the warmth of the car, steaming up the windows and fuzzing up the rear-view mirror.

By the time you get back to the house, there's hysteria. Izzy is failing to corral Ollie and Rob. She's brittle, they're frenzied, but in different ways – Ollie is frantic, three friends coming for a party is overwhelming when two years ago twenty-five little boys in a soft play area would have been a monthly, mundane, occurrence. Rob (Robert Alan, named for his grandfather and his father) is overwrought because he's being sent to his maternal grandparents after breakfast so as not to over-crowd the house. Breakfast – the pivot point of the day – has been waiting for you. They have been waiting for you.

Izzy says nothing, but the mantis-bird looks sharper than ever, as if she'd happily grab you with spiked arms and bite your head off. Probably that wouldn't even hurt – don't they paralyse their prey first?

It's not until Rob has been collected, bawling and teary, the party table laid, the cake put on display and the (biodegradable) birthday banner hung on the wall that you get to offer an apology for disappearing without warning.

Izzy just stares at you. "Why the hell—"

Before she can continue the first boy shows up, with a pushy mum who literally shoulders you out of the way and commandeers Izzy, talking about socially distanced games. Ironic, given that she just body-blocked you. Even more ironic, you felt something – not pain, but a definite unpleasant sensation. Two more mums, both of whom depart rapidly, and two more boys. The house vibrates with running feet, yelling voices, the strange smell of biscuits and pencil shavings that typifies pre-pubescent boys.

So it's late afternoon before it's all over. Pushy mum stayed the whole time, making the boys sit equidistantly round the table like points of the compass, cleaning her own son's hands with wet wipes whenever he touches anything other than his own plate and plastic tumbler and goody bag. Izzy sips herbal tea, although maybe she's spiked it with something, given how much of it she gets down her – three trips to the kettle in two hours, by your count.

Rob comes back, scarlet and bawling, this time because he has to leave his grandparents and doesn't want to. Ollie slinks off to his room with a comic book that his mother is almost certainly going to confiscate by bedtime. You and Izzy poke through her freezer, you as if freezers hold no interest for you, and agree to order a take-away. The apology never gets made.

Now you're in countdown mode; each hour takes you closer to the post-breakfast departure. No sleep again, but you tough it out, keeping your feet in the bed and your mind focused on the drive home. Silence, good take-away coffee, efficiency.

Izzy pecks you goodbye, but doesn't draw blood. Ollie gives you a hug, Rob, predictably, screams his head off.

You get the coffee, you drive efficiently. All the way home you can feel it, especially around your armpits, a rough itchiness that's only half painful. If you lift your arm to your mouth, you can taste it, the salt ocean, crusting your skin, abrading every joint and angle of your body. It's in your hairline, although you stuck your head under the tap to remove the obvious evidence of saltiness from your hair. It was there all through Oliver's party, intensifying its effect on your body, itching and inflaming everywhere that your clothing rubbed. All night, a faint stickiness, gluing you to your nightclothes. Every move an adhesion, a peeling away a part of you from something. After another day and night there will be reddening, roughening, irritation, inflammation. Aliveness.

You can reach down and scratch your calves, leaving dry white lines that fade slowly from your skin. You can shove your fingers into your hair and hear the crackle of salt-roots being pried apart. There's a mineral smell, as if the ocean inhabits you, allied to the chemical odour of deodorant that you've used to mask the evidence that you haven't showered since you swam.

The longest you've gone is six days. Obviously you wash bits of you, you're not slovenly: your groin and feet and teeth and eventually armpits, although you can do three days easy with roll-on deodorant. On the fourth day though, the backs of your pits will start to flay themselves on your bra straps.

Your phone rings. Mum and Dad. You put them on speakerphone and make anodyne conversation about Ollie's party and Rob's time with his other grandparents. Your parents don't see Izzy and the kids at present; your Dad's vulnerable – COPD – and every member of your family knows about fragility and loss now.

Alan had a ruptured brain aneurysm. He survived two days in hospital apparently, although nobody gets to see him there. Izzy found him on the floor at home, passed out. He never came round. During the pandemic this kind of thing was anomalous, inexplicable. People masked and gloved and distanced and vaccinated – this should have been protection but Alan, with no family history and no warning signs, died of something nobody in the family had ever heard of.

Izzy made the boys stay upstairs until the ambulance came. You can imagine that sharp-edged figure at the foot of the stairs; menacing. But of course she wouldn't have been there, she would have been on the kitchen floor with Alan's head in her prickly lap. Eventually your parents hang up and silence returns. You take your hand from the wheel and lick the inside of your arm. Still salt.

The coffee is cold. The car too hot. The noise of the tyres on the road is soporific. You pinch the bridge of your nose until your eyes water. Vigilance, that's what you need, although if Alan is an example, vigilance is pointless.

You remember Rob's wet face, the constant anguish of his frustration and fear. It's a more honest way to deal with grief than Izzy's, or yours, but you can't force sorrow any more than you can predict disaster. You can stare into the darkness and death comes at you out of the light. The pointlessness of your own life, when Alan had so much to live for, is tsunami-like. Not the great crashing wave but the drawing back that precedes the wall of water – the gasping fish, the exposed ribs of the ocean floor, the great stinking territory over which the disaster will advance.

You shrug your shoulders, feeling microscopic salt flakes shiver down your spine. When it comes, you'll be ready. Until then, you just need to practice pretending to feel.

BIAFRA IN PICTURES
Nwanne Agwu

the pictures are of Biafra.
in black & white,
the dichotomy of evil & good.

held away from your body, you
stare at each picture like a stain
of sin, ready to put your future
in the place of your history.

i.

a boy smiles with hands
on his waist. you count his
ribs, thinking which one
could form Eve & why
a skeleton is potbellied?

you check the colour of his
hair and do not know if in
a world of two extremities
the otherworldly is a mixture
of both or a presentation of
none. you think of grey as the
boy's hair, equating it to a
malnourished body. his smile
is cold. a disinterested gaze
onto the distance behind the
camera. under his eyes are
dark mounds, the earth
at the graves of his parents.

behind him is a church
with broken windows. you think of
chapels, of unanswered prayers,
of the noise in solitude, the fear
in the boy's eyes, the sadness.

ii.

in the crook of her arm,
a woman holds her baby.
headless, the body is.
on its mother's feet, the
baby's sweet face smiles,
shaved head glistening like
oil under the sun.

you seek the definition of
pietà on her face, watching
to find anger locked inside
her eyes, under her breath.

iii.

a boy lies in his blood.
in your mind's eye, he floats,
his blood is a pool shading
the green of his uniform.
"oga soldier," a girl calls him,
he answers with silence.

you think of soft things, of exposure,
of loss, of nothing, of something.

you pick up beer and it's not for minors.
porn says 18+. still, you go on.

you step back into the pictures
and…

iv.

your eyes
are on the ground,
counting shadows. blindness
is the absence of sun/light.

a girl walks in with her
head of hair grown into a bush,
collecting dust & lice.

by her sides,
the spindly hands & legs
of a baby are thrown askance,
a strip of fabric fastens
one human to the other.

below her skirt,
a leg ends at the ankle.
another testimony like her baby,
like her streaming eyes. at night,
she is in your dream, a bird
under the rain, flightless.

v.

you shut your eyes,
there's more to see.
you shut your eyes,
there's none to see.
evil takes your hand.
evil leads you away.

The Hiding Place
Meg Eden

A woman is not a body, I tell myself
when it is dark & I'm afraid.

How little I know what it means
to suffer in the darkest roots & hollows

of myself—how greatly I fear
my mint-sealed body opened like a box.

At night, I'm haunted by Betsie Ten Boom,
stripped naked into showers with strangers,

her skin made uniform, marching in the cold—
Betsie Ten Boom, crawling

over dead bodies to get to the toilet,
Betsie Ten Boom added to the bodies.

Her belongings sealed in a bag
at her arrival, Betsie had nothing

to hide behind. It was that nakedness
I feared at twelve years old—not

Nazis nor illness, not labor
nor death. In my mind

I killed Nazis with my bare hands.
I built shelters to hide Jews.

In all my stories I was the one
with power—but what power

did Betsie have in her nakedness?
The way she rested *in the sanctuary*

of God's fleas brings the fear
of what God might ask from me.

How He might strip me clean of me
& ask that still—despite—I keep my joy.

"BAR BAR"
Greg Delanty

"Let me say it openly: we are surrounded by an enterprise of degradation, cruelty,
and killing which rivals anything that the Third Reich was capable of, indeed dwarfs
it, in that ours is an enterprise without end, self-regenerating, bringing rabbits, rats,
poultry, livestock ceaselessly into the world for the purpose of killing them."
— J.M. Coetzee, from *The Lives of the Animals*

The lecturer quotes Adorno, "Writing poetry
after Auschwitz is barbaric".
Barbarous to compare this atrocity

with that, reduce each to the generic,
but consider, say, what many of us wear,
what most daily eat and drink, our trick

of general tergiverse everywhere.
How was your beef, salmon, veal?
Have you ever visited a farm anywhere?

Surely pigs can't really think or feel?
Then there's testing mice, monkey and chick
for the sake of curing a child. A lousy deal

for creatures. Excuse me waxing didactic.
If this is poetry then it's nothing bar barbaric.

Note: The languages non-Greek speakers spoke sounded to Greeks like "bar bar", thus barbarian.

MY POETRY ISN'T ART ENOUGH
Pragya Gogoi

Last evening, I wrote a poem
About girls whose skin smelled of earth and herbs,
Petrichor and marigolds – raw, beautiful, divine,
And contemplated the pages reduce to cinders
In the bonfire at my backyard.
You see, I burn poems each night
It's a ritual to mollify my embitterment
For I know not how to be a poet.
My mind is a high tide of words hitting the shores
And yet my brain fizzles out to extricate them
To conceive poetry that is art enough.
I can't weave poetry in knitted jumpers to warm your icy skin.
I haven't fallen in love in decades
to serve you poems garnished with wild kisses.
My soul, you know,
is bereft of metaphors to festoon mundane poems.
I know not the number of times I served unpunctuated poetry on paper
Almost like disproportionate apple slices on the periphery of the chinaware.
I can't remember ideas impregnating my mind at night the following dawn.
They evanesce as swiftly as they glide into my brain,
At times leaving footprints that I later give shape into unfinished poetry.
I don't see stardust in the bones of people like poets do
Or find poems carrying the weight of patriarchy in Mom's saree folds.
I haven't stayed up long enough on dark rainy nights
To pour buckets of poignant memories on paper at 2am.
I fail to stitch poems with threads of heartbreak rolling out from your heart
Or embroider words of love on your burgundy wounds,
For I only possess a handful of words mixed with incorrect punctuations in a bowl
That taste like insipid pancakes without maple syrup.
And I have hence surmised,
My poetry isn't art enough.

CLOCK WEATHERING
Fred Johnston

Cold weather's at the door like a milkman with his bill
Some idiot child is setting off fireworks to scare the dogs
Two streets over you can get every sort of hash and pill
From a hooded acne-victim who takes your cash and jogs
Into the faintly astringent dark, full of his own importance
As if this were a real job and a certain respect was due
I know nothing of this first-hand, of course, just by chance
You catch these little facts like a virus on the wind, you
Absorb them, and become immune. A flag of Palestine
Is struggling to stay aloof on a roof a few doors down
Every house is painted white-into-grey, until fine
Grains of salt driven up from the close-by sea ladle brown-
Red streaks like blood-spills from news videos down the wall
Cold weather's at the door like a milkman with his bill
The sky folds in low as a shroud and you just manage to crawl
Under it; there's someone in the kitchen – keep very still.

Christmas Eve, 1963
Thomas McCarthy

My holy family was down on its December luck, but I was not

As I delivered a Christmas number of *The Daily Mail*
To Miss Cliffe whose father had first reported upon
Our Blessed Lady at Knock. Christmas had come again without fail
As I knew it would. It was one of the eternal promises
Of Fianna Fáil that even the poorest might avail
Of Christmas: maybe even more than once a year, given
The way our Tariff Economy was booming. Light traces

Of snow peppered my fairly worn hand-me-down coat,
My knuckles were cold with a cold that wouldn't go
Away until maybe 1972 or '73, so there would be ten years of it
From that blue afternoon outside Miss Cliffe's door.
Being cold helps a child to concentrate on the strange sight
Of others being happy, houses where other children are not so poor.
I was living vicariously off Christmases seen behind glass

Like one of the Magi in the blue dark. Late, but nearer the light.

THE SOUTHWORD INTERVIEW
Thomas McCarthy, Poet

Thomas McCarthy was born in Cappoquin, County Waterford, in 1954. Educated at the local Convent of Mercy and at University College Cork, he was a Fellow of the International Writing Program in Iowa in 1978/79. He worked at Cork City Libraries until 2014 when he withdrew to write full-time. He has published ten collections of poetry including *The Sorrow Garden* (1981), *The Last Geraldine Officer* (2009), *Pandemonium* (2016) and *Prophecy* (2019) as well as two novels and two books of non-fiction. His prose-book, *Poetry, Memory and the Party*, was published by Gallery Press in 2021. Awards include The Patrick Kavanagh Award, The Alice Hunt Bartlett Prize, The Lawrence O'Shaughnessy Award for Poetry and the Annual Literary Award of the Ireland Funds. A member of Aosdána, he lives in Cork City.

The following interview was given with Patrick Cotter in 2022.

Unlike many of the working-class poets of your generation you had a childhood/adolescence more culturally complex than average. Can you tell us a little about that?

The complexity of this situation is entirely a function of where I was born poor – in Cappoquin, a small town on the banks of the tidal Blackwater, an immensely rich countryside with a thriving economy when I was a child. I understood very quickly that the poverty of my family was due to peculiarities and shortcomings in my own family, that it wasn't anyone else's fault. I worked like a dog from about the age of nine, delivering newspapers before school and delivering milk before I delivered the newspapers. My father was idle and ill for nearly all of my childhood, so the only money coming into the house were small weekly welfare cheques. I blamed nobody for this except my father who spent what little money my mother had saved on endless correspondence courses, in accountancy, engineering and art. My father would talk to my older brother Michael and me about his various 'correspondence' materials, whether in business studies or art. He imparted tons of cultural information to Michael and me, giving us a lifelong love of art, the art market, and strange things like company Annual Reports, etc. I think Michael and I got a hilarious home education in these things from our bone idle and depressive father. Then I joined Fianna Fáil to defy my father, and everybody else. My father was a closet communist, a cynic. From the age of nine I had no intention of becoming either. I could see how hard people were working in Cappoquin, in the Bacon Factory, in the Knockmeal Co-Op and in O'Connors' Chickens. I thought that there were amazing opportunities in Ireland for those willing to do a day's work. Then I joined the local library, then I started gardening. It was gardening in a way that led me into the wider world of books – through gardening first for wealthy Americans who had leased the beautiful dower-house of Sir Richard Keane's family and then for Brigadier FitzGerald who really became a lifelong friend. Brigadier FitzGerald, a retired army officer and Partner of the Panmure Gordon stockbrokers, was simply blown away that his young gardener had (a) read most of Molly Keane's then unknown novels and Dervla Murphy's books (b) could understand a balance-sheet and had read Annual Reports of Public Companies and (c) was writing poems and had published poems in the local school magazine. But also, that I knew how to propagate *Kalmia latifolia* by air-layering. The fact is, I was absolutely interested in absolutely everything, and had got all my information either from my father or from the Public Librarian in Cappoquin, Mrs. Bolger. That certainly hasn't changed. Our poverty never worried me as a child; I was supremely confident that I'd escape it. Absolutely confident. It was the 1960s, you must remember, Ireland was getting better and better. Let me tell you something about my competitive mental state at that time. When I was twelve our teacher told us that Minister O'Malley intended to bring in Free Secondary Education for everyone. I was absolutely disgusted because I was already looking forward to competing for a Scholarship with the Christian Brothers in Lismore. The idea that everyone in my class, all the idlers and idiots who never got 90% in their tests, would also be able to get into the same Secondary School horrified me. The word 'complex' hardly covers my 1960s working-class mental state, but I was a complex little boy.

The poems you published in the school magazine – why poems and not gardening articles? Were you reading any living poets at that stage?

I was acutely aware that Cappoquin had always produced poets, poets such as Pádraig Denn and Michael Cavanagh. Denn wrote in Irish and also translated *the New Testament* into Irish as part of a counterblast against the work of the Bible Societies in Irish-speaking areas; he also edited Sullivan's *Pious Miscellany*, a best-selling poetry book of the early Nineteenth Century. Cavanagh was a Fenian poet who fled to America and became the Editor of a Washington newspaper. I didn't know then that Joyce had mentioned Cappoquin in his *Ulysses* ("Cappoquin he came from he said on the Blackwater but it was too short then the day before he left May yes it was May when the infant king of Spain was born" (*Ulysses*, p681, Penguin, 1976). Molly Bloom's would-be lover on that Rock of Gibralter was a Lieutenant Mulvey of Cappoquin. Anyway, I didn't know any of that, but I knew that Cappoquin produced poets. When I was 15 in St. Anne's, the Convent of Mercy

Secondary School at Cappoquin, our then English teacher, Sr. Carmel, organised a school magazine *THE GOLDEN FLEECE* and appointed me as Editor. I don't think we had any gardening feature at all, but we were short of poems so I wrote two. That was Oct/Nov of 1969. I haven't stopped writing poems since that month in '69. As usual, I wrote a lot before it occurred to me that there might be poetry books in the local library. So I found them, a Selected Thom Gunn and Ted Hughes from Faber and a copy of Richard Murphy's *Sailing to an Island*. At Christmas that year, or it may have been January 1970, I got my hands on a copy of *The Young British Poets*, with Seamus Heaney within its covers.

Did Heaney from the first speak to you? I can imagine Ted Hughes's country fauna appealing to a Cappoquin boy, but Gunn's work must have been a bit of a mystery.

I don't think I took Heaney really seriously until *North* in 1975. The sheer authority of that book blew me away and it was confirmed a few year later by *Field Work*. But in those very early years Richard Murphy was my poet, without a doubt. Gunn's work I took to because he wrote motorbike poems and I had a Honda 90. I thought the violence in Hughes's animal poems was terrific. But a lot of those achievements went over my head. I was just too romantic, too Victorian, in my tastes at that stage. I was very unmodern.

The Romantic and the Victorian were common characteristics of every tyro poet at that time, I think. Were you appreciating any of Yeats by now?

I should have mentioned Yeats earlier! He was the giant in my youthful imagination, the cultural equivalent of the political de Valera. For me the two of them were the embodiment of the House of Imagination as created by Fenians, IRB men, patriots and heroes. That Yeats wrote about the Big Houses, where I was working trying to restore a damn falling-down garden, only deepened the sincerity of his voice for me. There was a Collected Yeats in the Cappoquin Library, I devoured that at 17 and 18 before I went to college.

Did you differentiate at that stage between 'the Lake Isle of Inisfree' and 'Sailing to Byzantium'? Were you able to discern the seismic change in style, in sensibility, in complexity? At what time did you become aware that the Romantic & Victorian would not do and change your own poems?

I wrote as if I had read only 'the Lake Isle of Innisfree', but I understood how powerful 'Sailing to Byzantium' was, and I was delighted that Yeats had written 'Among School Children' after a visit to the Ursulines in Waterford. I understood, I mean both intellectually and tonally, the difference between the early Yeats and the mature Yeats but I was wedded to romance and anti-modern lyricism until the early 90s when I started writing the poems that went into *The Lost Province*. In my poetry-writing life everything is either before or after 1996.

It was very much Yeats the Public Man which seemed to influence the poems of The First Convention, *not just in subject matter, but in rhetorical flourish, a flourish absent from others of your UCC coevals. Theo Dorgan had a declamatory style influenced by Graves perhaps and Sean Dunne had an unshakeable attachment to repetitive iambs.*

It was the presumption of authority in Yeats' voice that really thrilled me. I believed it, and the more I learned about Yeats the more I understood how he held that presumption of moral leadership through poetry. He had earned it, he had simply paid more attention to the details of Irish politics and Irish history than any other poet. Despite all his mythologising and his magic gobbledegook, he felt a duty to lead because he knew he had command of many facts. It always struck me that he had command of facts in the way his father, JBY, merely had command of many prejudices and witticisms. WB's command always impressed me. I felt it gave all poets license to speak in such a manner. But some poets are intensely private and have no wish to comment on the public realm. Fair enough, I honour that kind of poet too. But before I reached the age of 60, I wouldn't have spent much time reading such work.

Personally, I would make a distinction between authority of (literary) voice and authority of opinion. Yeats asserted both. Tell me about the first poems you placed in recognised literary outlets. Who saw them before you submitted them? Did you submit many poems to such outlets which were rejected before the first were accepted, or were the first you submitted 'oven-ready'?

That's interesting, I mean what you say there. I see no distinction between authority of literary voice and authority of opinion. Sometimes the idleness of an irresponsible opinion can be fuel – pure petroleum – in poetry. The amazing thing is that artists can hold bizarre opinions for such a long time, withstanding both mature insight and re-education because of the implacable position that their impulse to write has placed them in. History moves on, sometimes writers don't. They remain stuck where they began. My first poems were published in the school magazine in 1969 when I was fifteen. They were written out of necessity. Our English teacher, Sr. Carmel, asked if someone could please write a few poems for the Christmas issue of the magazine, saying it was a disgrace that there were no poems when the town of Cappoquin was famous for its poets. I obliged by writing two poems. Then I began showing my poems to WED Allen, an Anglo-Irishman who was a Russian scholar and historian and his friend, Dervla Murphy, whom I visited regularly in Lismore. Dervla showed some of my poems to her then lover Terence deVere White, then Literary Editor of *the Irish Times*. Terence wrote to me to say that he was going to publish one of my poems in the *IT* Saturday page. So I had a poem in *the Irish Times* when I was seventeen. But I started sending poems to English magazines like *Outlook* and to *New Irish Writing* in the Irish Press, without success. I didn't have a poem in *New Irish Writing* until 1977, the year I won the Patrick Kavanagh Award. But I kept sending poems out, most of the time collecting rejection slips, but now and again striking gold.

I find it amazing that the poems of The First Convention *did not more easily find periodical homes. Was it after you won the award that the majority of the poems began to be accepted?*

In the mid Seventies *The Cork Examiner* had a 'New Poetry' feature, established by Gerry Fitzgibbon of UCC, and a number of my earliest poems were published in that column – with commentary, which was very uplifting. I also had poems in *Icarus,* then edited by Maurice Scully, and *Cyphers* published some poems. As well as that poems were published in *Quarryman,* the great UCC literary journal, and in *FIRST ISSUE* edited by William Wall. So I didn't feel blocked or frustrated in any way when I was a student poet. I dined out as a student on having been published in *The Irish Times* before I even got to college. Interestingly, Terence de Vere White didn't publish me again for four years, until he published 'Her Blindness,' 'Death By Fire' and 'State Funeral' in 1975 and 1976. He wrote to me about those poems and his enthusiasm meant a lot to me. But I do remember being envious of a College poet, the late John O'Mahony of Dunmanway, who seemed to be effortlessly accepted by David Marcus at *New Irish Writing* in *The Irish Press.* John's quick success with David did annoy me! The funny thing is, I seemed to be the only College poet who was sending stuff out with determined regularity. The others, whether Maurice Riordan, Gregory O'Donoghue or Theo Dorgan, didn't seem to be that pushed about publishing. If a new poem won the approval and praise of John Montague that was almost as good as being published: that was the general feeling on campus, I think.

David did great work for the short story, and in founding the journal Poetry Ireland, *but didn't seem that gifted as a poetry editor. How much of Montague's opinions on your work did you take notice of?*

I had huge respect for Montague's opinion on all poems, on every kind of poetry. He had produced the goods, those exquisite Dolmen publications like *Tides* and *The Rough Field,* and the earlier classics from McGibbon and Kee like *Poisoned Lands* and *A Chosen Light.* I was delighted by the world of *A Chosen Light* when I got a copy of it in 1975 or '76. It is a completely seductive book with that killer-combination of French life and Irish history: Ulster and Paris, for God's sake how could he not be impressive? By 1976, I'd say, I had such a good understanding of Montague that I knew which poems not to show him. That's an important moment for a poet: when you realize your own territory is more important than any master's territory. It's not something you'd want to divulge immediately, well, not until the poems are safely published and can't be changed. As a young poet you wish to hand a published book to a mentor, expressing regrets for straying from the received opinion. From '76 on I was sure of my own road, I could see it lying ahead.

What did it mean to you to win the Kavanagh Award and be published by Dolmen in particular?

It meant everything to win the Kavanagh Award. We had studied Patrick Kavanagh very carefully at secondary school, so I knew all the great poems. The Award itself, believe it or not, changed my life. There was an extraordinary amount of publicity about it that year, I was featured by Ciarán Carty in *the Sunday Independent*, interviewed by a slightly bemused Eavan Boland on RTÉ Radio One and my photo seemed to be in every national newspaper. I even got a letter of congrats from Lady Beit at Russborough House and she became a great correspondent over the years. Then I received letters from three different publishers. But I'd already sent the manuscript to Liam Miller at Dolmen Press, so he wrote immediately to say he'd publish the collection. He complained about too much enjambment in the poems and wanted me to deal with that. I didn't, but he still published the book in June 1978, less than a year after the Award. It is impossible to exaggerate the effect of this Award on my life. It set in motion a whole series of positive dominoes falling into my life, and these kept falling for at least seven more years; so I was nominated for the Iowa International Writing Program where I met the legendary Paul Engle, but where I also met Peter Jay of Anvil Press Poetry. Public mentions of Iowa brought me to the attention of Bryan MacMahon who had taught fiction at the Iowa workshop, so Bryan contacted me and got me to read at Listowel Writers' Week and to direct the Listowel Creative Writing Workshop. Peter Jay published my next book, *The Sorrow Garden*, that won the Alice Hunt Bartlett Prize in 1981, then three years later I won the Annual Literary Award of the Ireland Funds, a huge prize. That year I published *The Non-Aligned Storyteller* with Anvil Press. So it really was a sensational seven years, those seven years after my father died. My father had died in 1977, six months before the Kavanagh. I always regretted that he missed that. It would have meant everything to him.

This raises two questions. How did you cope with the next seven years when the limelight was not as bright and what is one to make of these days when national radio, the daily newspapers etc. couldn't be pushed to give such coverage to a literary award originating in Ireland? I have some cognisance of Mitteleuropa where the media still will report, with enthusiasm, national prizes and literary activities, as if they were as important as sport.

The next seven years after that were child-rearing years after Kate-Inez and Neil were born. Catherine and I just folded into ourselves and became completely family-centred, school-centred, and, I think, as happy as the day was long. I had so much spare voltage after those early modestly successful years that they've kept me going ever since.

Seven good years is more than any artist should expect in their lives. Other poets of my generation in UCC didn't get the same attention, I felt. Certainly, not so early in their published life. I don't know why because they were all both very good and very interesting in their own peculiar, particular ways. So I've always felt lucky, and I've certainly never felt neglected. Obviously, there are higher levels of fame, if you like, American and international fame – but you must understand – and everyone reading this should understand – that that takes a huge amount of work, of constant travel to attend festivals, etc. I have to be honest with you, I'd prefer to be gardening. I began as a gardener and gardening is an essential part of life for me. I tend to view everything through plants, even politics. We do now live in a very Balkanised cultural world where achievement isn't shared as quickly or universally in the media. But we are well-known in our own hermetic area within our cities or counties, like book-restorers or those who study lichens. I mean, how necessary is it to be known? I'm not at all convinced that it's necessary. As I've said, there is voltage to be had in wide publicity within the book trade, but it's not necessary. In fact, it can create an illusion both in the writers and in his or her readers. That being said, it's amazing how much effort you have to put into selling just 700 or 800 books. And that number of sales is a permanent tipping point, a monitor as to whether you have a pulse or not, in the poetry world.

I would be more concerned about the attention the work receives rather than the poet. For those concerned with attention for the person there is always the screaming marketplace of social media. What brought about the change, you touched upon earlier, in the lead up to The Lost Province?

Five years elapsed between *The Non-Aligned Storyteller* and *Seven Winters In Paris,* and six years then went by before I published *The Lost Province.* For most of those twelve years between 1984 and 1996 I was coasting along. I don't think the technique in my poems improved at all. Then I spent the years 1994-1995 teaching poetry and politics at Macalester College in Minnesota. That teaching year was crucial because I wrote with less idleness, with more an awareness of tone, verse structure and just a general sharpness. I remember re-writing entire poems so that they had a lyric verse structure, rhyming quatrains and not such casual, arbitrary line-breaks, etc. The awareness of verse-structure was part of a greater alertness to technique and tone. Interestingly, when I submitted the manuscript of *The Lost Province* to Anvil, Peter Jay had just taken leave so that Bill Swainson was in the editor's chair. He was impressed by the change of tone, the quickening of the technique. He thought it was my best book by far and that meant a lot to me. It was just about time to become sharper; to become sharper or decline as a poet worth reading.

Did throwing a critical eye over the work of students contribute to an awareness of the room for improvement in your own work?

Not just looking at the work of students but looking closely at the materials I was teaching. My 'Poetry and Politics' class at Macalester included work by Yeats, Auden, Lowell, Heaney and Nuala Ní Dhómhnaill, but also more ideological texts in the work of Pádraig Pearse, John Cornford, Father James Berrigan and Gerry Adams. The purpose of those fourteen classes was to compare and contrast the literary achievement of the work itself, including its technical failures, and its relationship with ideologies like Communism and Nationalism. Inevitably we went back to looking at Andrew Marvell on Cromwell and comparing that writing with the Irish patriotic and 'Aisling' poems. We really looked at Lowell closely in *Notebook* and the atmosphere of the Vietnam anti-war protests. It's worth quoting a four-liner from 'Charles River' in *Notebook*:

> 'If the clock had stopped in 1936
> for them, or again in '50 and '54 —
> they are not dead, and not until death parts us,
> will I stop sucking my blood from their hurt'

It's not that particular technical successes of those master-poets changed my thinking, but investigating the political purpose and tone of literary language in an academic context became a kind of abrupt reminder that writing is not passive. You can't just coast along, writing is a permanent agitation as in Lowell above, so that in thinking of our parents we are also embracing greater crises beyond them. This is more than verse-craft, it is 'voice,' the real, full thing. Teaching a full academic load of five courses in one year was a kind of sudden boot-camp. I shredded and re-wrote almost every poem in *The Lost Province* after that experience. I also spent endless hours with Mac's Professor John Bernstein whose Princeton Ph.D. had been done on Joseph Conrad and language. John became an amazing friend and mentor. He was a sharp reader of poetry and read everything.

But making changes at the level of "a lyric verse structure, rhyming quatrains and not such casual, arbitrary line-breaks, etc." could be done without consideration of how masters handle content. Did your reading of submissions for Poetry Ireland Review *as editor grant you any insight in how to write a better poem — at least before submission?*

I don't agree. How masters handle content is precisely how poems are made. Even if you wanted to use only iambic pentameter and abba rhyme, that technical decision is made earlier than we think. It is further back in your mind, further back than a knowledge of verse-craft — which is, after all, only craft. There's some life before the making of a poem, a meta-life, if you like; it must be similar to music, a kind of humming, murmurs of ideas taking a form. I trust that beforehand nature in writing. It is not reason, hardly reason at all, but something richer and more personal. Reading vast numbers of poems for a journal is no help at all, if anything it's a huge hindrance to one's personal work.

Tell me about Fianna Fáil. What were your intentions with the party poems? What did you think of the varying critical reactions?

Ah, what can a person say about FF that hasn't been said in some way before? It is such nebulous material, this public realm of feeling. It should generally be avoided by poets, but poets are inevitably drawn to this realm. What fascinated me about FF was that it seemed so un-poetic, anti-poetic even. I grew up in a working-class family (sub working-class really because for a good stretch of my childhood my father was ill and we lived on welfare). Some of my Bray relatives in Mount Melleray, small farmers and workers at the Abbey, my grand-uncle especially, were serious FF people, by this I mean 'The Party' came first – in everything, in choice of friends, in views of history, in devotion to de Valera 'The Chief', in which newspapers one read (*The Irish Press, Evening Press* and *Sunday Press,* owned by the de Valera family). These were not marginal papers – *the Sunday Press* had a Sunday circulation of 400,000. The Party had an atmosphere when I was growing up, a sense of owning the future as well as the past, a sense of optimism about Ireland and the Irish that penetrated into even working-class lives. The sociology of this fascinated me, it really did, its combination of Lemass business types in the cities, the industrial workers of tariff-protected industries (almost the entirety of Cork Harbour as well as Santry, Rialto in Dublin and the Shannon region; and that great horde of 500,000 agricultural labourers, many of whom left for English cities as agriculture was mechanised. The Party was a world. I began to write poems about it so that I could make sense of it. By the time I reached UCC and began to take the writing of poetry really seriously the Party had receded somewhat. The Ulster Troubles were a huge challenge to its inherent contradictions. Ulster ruined FF by testing its ideas. From the poetry point of view I had Theodore Roethke in mind and his 'greenhouse poems' about life among the florists of his father's glasshouses in the Saginaw Valley. John Montague and I discussed Roethke a lot, and I thought: well, if Roethke can write a sequence of more than ten poems about his father's floral business, then surely I can write about FF, its meetings and committees, its electioneering and parish-pump activities. So I tried to do that, beginning with de Valera's funeral in 'State Funeral' and then moving in closer to the actual material I remembered in early poems like 'The First Convention' and 'Last Days in the Party.' I kept circling round the hothouse of FF for years, so that even my third collection *The Non-Aligned Storyteller* is peppered with FF material like 'Shopkeepers at the Party Meeting' and 'The Chairman's Widow' and 'The President's Men.' The tone of the latter poem gets closest to the tone Roethke has in his greenhouse poems. So it was all just part of a single fascination, everything was integrated in that obsession: the Party, history, West Waterford, childhood, the absent father, the troubled father, etc.

The critical reaction to these poems annoyed me at the time, but now I can see that my annoyance was based on a lack of understanding of just how 'toxic,' how 'uncouth' this material is considered. Educated people, sensitive people, the very readership of poetry, feel appalled by these materials; educated people wondered why a person would even write about such things. The commentary was patronising in the extreme and certain commentators have maintained a patronising attitude to my work even now. But you write about what fascinates you, whether it's FF or the Anglo-Irish Big Houses in the same FF hinterland. You just write about what you know about. It is something you can do nothing about. We are stuck with our individual pasts, there's no way out.

All of your books have included what Eiléan Ní Chuilleanáin has described as 'the independent lyric' but right up until Prophecy *each of your books appeared to be dominated by poems driven by a particular paradigm. Were the poems related to one another coming into the world in a creative flow or were you deliberately setting out to write poems which fitted the various paradigms? Could you elaborate a little on each book's paradigm? Many poets, of course, assert retrospectively a common paradigm on groups of independently composed poems before going to print.*

I'm not sure about particular paradigms, I think more of particular obsessions. I have a habit of forming very long obsessions and these obsessions dominate my thinking for years at a time. Therefore 'the Party' was an early obsession, a very early one – I was writing a play called 'The Local Election' when I was eighteen and I was obsessively note-taking, making notes to myself. Poems like 'The First Convention' and 'Last Days in the Party' came out of that obsession. Then there was the image of de Valera that lingered long after his funeral in the mid-Seventies. Then there was the obsessive grief over the early deaths of my father and mother. The rage I felt over that, rage I never adequately dealt with at the time. But that obsession led to the poems in *The Sorrow Garden*. Then there was my obsession with the idea of a poet as a kind of disinterested photographer of history, a chronicler. Poems around that obsession are in *The Non-Aligned Storyteller* and *Seven Winters In Paris*. Then there were the two great obsessions that consumed nearly twenty years of my thinking and obsessing – the idea of a Catholic thriving through the Protestant Eighteenth century, surviving and enduring through trade and being connected with Catholic Europe. That was my Nathaniel Murphy, my *Merchant Prince*. My Nathaniel became so real my wife Catherine used to say, "Can I talk to you about something or are you talking to Nathaniel right now?" Nathaniel contained contradictions, a Catholic with a love of Protestant life, a provincial merchant with a cosmopolitan Roman outlook, a merchant yet a poet. The same with Colonel Sir Gerald FitzGerald of *The Last Geraldine Officer*. This is a book that came out of my time at Glenshelane House near Cappoquin, Brigadier FitzGerald's house and garden where I worked as a student. I've confused memories of the actual Brigadier with the invented Sir Gerald but telling the story of an Irish language poet who wears a British uniform, of a Geraldine of historic pedigree thrown into the industrial morass of modern warfare, it was really important for me to tell that story, but only through poetry. So, that Anglo-Irish society and its easy connections with the Gaelic world impressed me no end as a possibility. It really was an obsession. The word paradigm seems too prescriptive, too limiting. It is more organic than that; it's obsessive and personal and a way of holding on to seemingly contradictory views of the world. To be able to contain contradictions, that seems to be the one great obsession.

During the course of this interview the judgements you express about your father, while arguably/possibly justified, appear contemptuous. That contempt is echoed in poems at the beginning of your latest collection Prophecy. *I have never taken note of it in previous books or in our conversations going back years. Is it the perspective of your own experience as a father, a man of responsibilities, the perspective of having lived to an older, wiser, more mature age than him which has caused these judgements to form or were you always so aware and judging of his self-indulgence? Certainly as a father myself I know there is no room to pander to one's own daydreams and desires for an easy life when children have to be provided for. But isn't this the life that many in the gentry and aristocracy lead? Was your father simply cursed by not having as much money as they had to underwrite his attempts at 'self-improvement' during his 'unemployment'?*

Well spotted, is all I can say. And your question is well stated. My contempt for my father's waste of his intelligence is something that has never abated. It is part of the weather of my life, since I was about seven years old. Unabated and undiminished. True, my father was born the son of an impoverished blind widow in a country with almost no opportunities for advancement. As a child I was annoyed with him for not having emigrated like many of my cousins and all the other unemployed of Cappoquin. The emigrant cousins seemed to be doing well, indeed one, having left school at 13 in Ireland went on to be night-school educated in England and became a design engineer with Jaguar in Coventry. I thought my father should have gone with him, but he didn't. Instead, he did a 'correspondence course' in engineering with the British Institute of Engineering Technology. Got his 'Diploma' and put it in the bottom drawer with all the other qualifications. He was simply too depressed and too lazy. As if to prove my point, my sister emigrated because she wanted to train to be a nurse – which she did. My father didn't bring her to the airport in 1973; but I did with the help of my old Fianna Fáil friend, John Fraher, and his locally famous Mercedes. I'll never forget that Dan-Air flight to Bristol leaving Cork airport. As we drove away that morning, I felt all the hopelessness of the un-connected poor in Ireland and my father's utter uselessness. But he was depressed, and he was receiving medical treatment for that depression, including two hospitalisations. My problem is I've never accepted the debilitating nature of his deep depression. Maybe there are reasons why I won't accept it. But don't ask me what they are because I absolutely don't have a clue. My heart was hardened against my father very early on. There is no going back, it is part of my life. As for your characterisation of the local Anglo-Irish aristocracy – the fact is, every Anglo-Irish person I knew in the Cappoquin and Lismore district was working like a dog, day and night, to make ends meet. Farming, herding, pig-rearing, hen-rearing, market-gardening, every Protestant I knew worked themselves to the bone. Man or woman, they hardly knew an hour of idleness between Monday and Saturday of every week. In this they were the antithesis of my father. Now, is it any wonder that I liked them.

Of course I can think of Catholic aristocrats who might better characterise my pen portrait. Prophecy *has its groupings of poems, about your parents, your love for your wife Catherine Coakley, Cork, our recent historical anniversaries etc. Unlike many of your books whose architecture depended on what you have described as 'obsessions'* Prophecy *is a more eclectic collection whose poems' overarching link is your own unmistakable sensibility. Were many of these poems written before* Pandemonium *or did their composition mostly follow it?*

Almost without exception, all the poems in *Prophecy* were written after the poems in *Pandemonium.* As a matter of interest, I've just taken down my big notebook now. I can see that 'There Once Was a Girl' was written while I was sitting in the Boole Library at UCC on January 19th, 2018. 'A Celtic Miscellany' was written in the same place a week later; that was published in *POETRY* in February of 2019. 'The Dead of Albuera,' about Desmond O'Grady making love on Ezra Pound's bed, was written on March 26th of 2018 too. 'Age and Creativity' was written in June of 2018 and published in *the Irish Times* that September. So nearly all of *Prophecy* was written in 2018. It was a great year for me, certainly.

Fabulous production for one year. In your notebooks did the initial notes, from the first, strive towards the poetic line or were they written as prose statements like many of Yeats' work?

I never write a prose version of something that might be a poem. If I've written a prose version of an event or a feeling it stays that way, as a piece of prose, a note. It seems extraordinary, but I hardly changed a word of those poems, from the moment they were written to the typescript I sent to Carcanet. They just arrived in the fullness of themselves. Sometimes, you're just in the zone, and that year I certainly was. It's not too long ago, so I live in hopes that that feeling of poetic epiphany will come back to me yet again! I may have to return to the Boole Library. Sometimes walking in the UCC campus has that effect on me: the feeling of springtime, the youthfulness of the poetic impulse, rushes back to me as if I was twenty years old and I had all the time in the world.

THE GREGORY O'DONOGHUE
INTERNATIONAL POETRY COMPETITION

Judge: Suji Kwock Kim

1st Prize:
€2,000
Publication in *Southword* 44
Guest reading at the Cork International Poetry Festival
(with four-night hotel stay and full board)
Featured on the Southword Poetry Podcast

2nd Prize:
€500
Publication in *Southword* 44

3rd Prize:
€250
Publication in *Southword* 44

Ten runners-up will be published in *Southword* 44
and receive a €50 publication fee

The competition is open to original, unpublished poems in the English language of 40 lines or fewer. The poem can be on any subject, in any style, by a writer of any nationality, living anywhere in the world.

Deadline: 30th November, 2022
Guidelines: www.munsterlit.ie

Southword Literary Essay Competition

Judge: Patrick Cotter

1st Prize:
€1,000

8 Runners-Up:
€500

All nine essays will be published
over the course of 18 months
(next three issues of *Southword*)

The competition is open to original, unpublished, personal essays between 2500 – 5000 words. We're looking for personal, confessional essays which border on memoir – gripping essays full of memories and feelings. The best indicator of the kind of thing which interests us is what we have published in past issues; essays by Kim Addonizio, Sandra Beasley, Simon Van Booy, Carlo Geblér, Thomas Lynch, Anthony Walton, Helen Mort and Kim Moore.

Essays will be judged anonymously by editor Patrick Cotter.

There is an entry fee of €20.

Deadline: 28th February 2023
Guidelines: www.munsterlit.ie

CONTRIBUTORS

Nwanne Agwu is from Okposi and lives in Abakaliki, Nigeria. You can find him on Twitter @NwanneAgwu.

Gerard Beirne has published six books of fiction and poetry. His short story collection was shortlisted for the Danuta Gleed Literary Award.

Daragh Byrne is a Sydney-based Irish poet. In 2022, his work appeared in *Abridged, Skylight 47, Crannóg* and *Poetry London.*

Kevin Cahill is a poet from Cork. His work has recently appeared in *The New Statesman.*

Swiss-born, Scotland-based **Regi Claire** is a fiction writer and poet shortlisted for the Forward Prizes 2020 (Best Single Poem).

A renamed Dublin pub marked **Louise G. Cole**'s 2018 Hennessy win, followed by publication as Carol Ann Duffy's Laureate's Choice.

Deirdre Crowley is an artist and writer from West Cork. Publications include the *Ogham Stone* and The Bournemouth Writing Prize 2022.

John Paul Davies' work appears in *Banshee, Maine Review, Abridged, Apex, Southword (issue 37), Crannóg & Channel.* From Birkenhead, he lives in Navan. Twitter: @johndavies1978.

Tomás de Faoite was born in Dowth, Ireland and now lives in the Netherlands. His latest collection, *Winter Solstice* was published by Uitgeverij Van Kemenade in 2019.

Julia Deakin lives in West Yorkshire. Widely published, she edits *Pennine Platform* magazine and is working on her fifth collection.

Greg Delanty's latest collection is *No More Time.* An award winner; the National Library recently released his papers, see catalogue.nli.ie/Collection/vtls000820766.

Meg Eden is the author of the 2021 Towson Prize for Literature winning poetry collection *Drowning in the Floating World* (Press 53, 2020).

Michael Farry is a retired primary teacher. His latest poetry collection, *Troubles* (2020), is published by Revival Press, Limerick.

Tracy Gaughan is a writer and editor from Galway. She holds an MA in Comparative Literature.

Pragya Gogoi is an author and engineer from India. Winner of several awards, she is currently working on her second book.

Claire Hennessy is a writer, editor, and creative writing facilitator from Dublin.

David S. Higdon is a writer from Kentucky. His work has been published in *Appalachian Review, Still: The Journal,* and others.

Patrick Holloway is a prize-winning writer of stories and poems. He is an editor of *The Four Faced Liar.* Follow him on twitter @hollowaywriter2.

Olaitan Humble has been nominated for the Rhysling Award, Pushcart Prize and Best of the Net Award. His writing appears in *Fiyah, Hobart* and *Chiron Review,* among others.

Fred Johnston's most recent collection of poems is *Rogue States* (Salmon Poetry, 2019). Founder of Galway's annual Cúirt literature festival in 1986, he lives in Galway.

Anne Kennedy specialises in acrylics and watercolours. Her work was included in *The Welcome Branch* installation at the Glucksman, UCC in 2021, presented by the Lantern Project.

Róisín Leggett Bohan was chosen for Poetry Ireland's Introduction Series 2022. When she is not writing she might be seen searching for ghosts.

Fran Lock's most recent collections are *White/ Other* (The 87 Press, 2022) and *Hyena!* (Poetry Bus Press, 2022).

Lorraine McArdle was awarded the Poetry Collection Prize at Listowel Writers Week in 2022. She is published in *Poetry Ireland Review, The North, The Interpreter's House* and *Skylight 47.*

Martin Mc Carthy lives in Cork City, where he studied English at UCC. His latest collection is *Lockdown* (2021).

Thomas McCarthy's prose-book, *Poetry, Memory and the Party,* was published by Gallery Press in 2021.

Sinéad McClure's writing appears in *The Stinging Fly, Live Encounters, Ink, Sweat & Tears,* and in radio and other fine publications.

Alan McCormick lives in Wicklow. Recent work can also be read in the latest *Stinging Fly* and *Sonder* magazines. www.alanmccormickwriting.wordpress.com.

James McDermott's poetry books include *Manatomy* (Burning Eye), *Erased* (Polari Press) and *Green Apple Red* (Broken Sleep Books).

Afric McGlinchey's *Tied to the Wind* (Broken Sleep Books, 2021), a hybrid memoir, was awarded an Arts Council Literature Bursary.

Donal McLaughlin has published two collections of stories. In 2022, he was longlisted for the BBC National Short Story Award.

John Minihan was born in Dublin in 1946 and raised in Athy, County Kildare. His photographs have been exhibited throughout the world.

Geraldine Mitchell's most recent collection is *Mute/Unmute* (Arlen House, 2020). She lives on the Co Mayo coast.

Donna Morton's *Forbidden Flowers* (with Carmen Cornue) was a chapbook finalist for the Fool for Poetry Chapbook Competition and Host Publications. Instagram: @spleen1857.

Virginia native **Rebecca Moseman** has been exhibited throughout the US and abroad and has featured within *Black & White Magazine*, *GUP*, *Resource*, *DodHo*, and *SHOTS Magazine*.

David Murphy's most recent book, his sixth, is the debut poetry collection *Drowning in the Desert* published by Revival Press. Website: www.davidmurph.wordpress.com.

Lani O'Hanlon lives in West Waterford. Winner of the Poetry Ireland Trocaire Competition 2022, her poetry is published internationally.

Jane Robinson is the author of *Journey to the Sleeping Whale* (Salmon Poetry). Her next collection launches in March 2023.

Róisín Ryan is from County Limerick. Her writing has previously appeared in *Púca*. You can find her on Twitter @roisin_ni_riain.

Leah Saint Marie is a filmmaker living in Los Angeles, CA. She can be found writing poetry at Little Dom's in Los Feliz.

Kay Sexton has had over a hundred short stories published, along with two non-fiction books and a novel.

Jess Smith is currently an Assistant Professor of Practice at Texas Tech University. See more at www.jesselizabethsmith.com.

Trelawney's work has appeared in *Ink, Sweat and Tears,* Broken Sleep's anthology of Modern Cornish Poets and beyond. @bentrelawney.

Jose Varghese is a writer/translator and editor from India, working on his first novel and a collection of short stories.

Amy Woolard is an attorney living in Charlottesville, Virginia, USA. Her debut poetry collection *NECK OF THE WOODS* was published by Alice James Books in 2020.

How to Submit

Southword welcomes unsolicited submissions of original work in fiction and poetry during the following open submission periods:

POETRY

What to submit: Up to four poems in a single file
When to submit: 1st December, 2022 – 28th February, 2023
Payment: *Southword* will pay €40 per poem

FICTION

What to submit: One short story (no longer than 5,000 words)
When to submit: 1st January – 31st March, 2023
Payment: *Southword* will pay €250 for a short story of up to 5,000 words

Submissions will be accepted through our Submittable portal online.
Visit www.southword.submittable.com for further guidelines.

Printed in Great Britain
by Amazon